Under the Sign of the Lily

The Messianic Sophianic Age

Recognize and Heal Yourself
through the Power of the Spirit

Recognize and Heal Yourself through the Power of the Spirit

*The Eternal Word,
the One God, the Free Spirit,
speaks through Gabriele,
as through all the prophets of God –
Abraham, Moses, Isaiah, Job, Elijah,
Jesus of Nazareth, the Christ of God*

Gabriele
Publishing House

The Free Universal Spirit
Is the Teaching of the Love for God and Neighbor
toward Human Beings, Nature and Animals

Recognize and Heal Yourself
through the Power of the Spirit
3rd Edition, February 2020

© Gabriele-Verlag Das Wort GmbH
Max-Braun-Str. 2, 97828 Marktheidenfeld, Germany
www.gabriele-verlag.com
www.gabriele-publishing-house.com

Original German Title:
Erkenne und Heile Dich Selbst
durch die Kraft des Geistes

The German edition is the work of reference for all
questions regarding the meaning of the contents.

Translation authorized by
Gabriele-Verlag Das Wort GmbH

All rights reserved

Printed by: KlarDruck GmbH, Marktheidenfeld, Germany

Order No. S 102en
ISBN 978-3-96446-030-1

Table of Contents

Preface 17

Foreword 19

Part 1:
The Human Being as an Energy Field of the Spirit – The Right Way of Life to Stay Healthy and Spiritually Active

The positive or negative programming
in the morning is decisive 23

The spiritually knowing, positively attuned person .. 36

The law and impact of the holy, divine
ether powers 45

The willfulness of the fallen spirit beings led to
the condensation of matter, to the human being
with his illnesses and blows of fate 52

Lawful thoughts and actions lead back into
the energy field of the divine Spirit 56

The unfoldment of the "God-man" via the
purification of the soul and the expansion
of the ether body 62

Blessedness and well-being by the power
of thoughts 67

The spiritual forces are also healing forces
 that every human being can request 71

The correct use of the divine ether powers
that permeate all life forms 74

All that is condensed must be transformed 78

The one who wants to enter the Kingdom
 of God has to bring heaven with him 82

The effects of negative thoughts and
human conceptions 84

The reaction of the body cells to negative
thoughts and medications 87

Negative effects caused by the exploitation of
the Earth and technical achievements 90

Patience, persistence and devotion in prayers
for healing 92

The knowing person can make use of the
upbuilding odic forces of all life forms 98

Many radiations influence the energy fields
of human beings 102

Dead food and the heavenly elixir of life 105

The law of cause and effect 108

Killing and consuming animals leads to
soul burden 110

Incorrect preparation and usage of farmland 115

Animal foods develop sensuality, a hard heart
and brutality in human beings 117

Prayer releases energies –
Fanaticism causes harm 121

Self-chastisement does not dissolve cravings –
Repression and its incalculable consequences
for the soul 122

What vibrations adhere to animal products
and to organic foods? 125

Humankind is annihilating itself 131

The human being can regain his health only if
he abides by the laws of the Lord, also in
regard to the plant and animal kingdoms 133

Thoughtlessly treated natural products reduce
their energy-giving qualities 135

Especially high ether powers at sunrise are
active for human beings and the harvest 139

How can the vibration of "auxiliary food"
be built up? 141

The heart prayer and its actualization is the
highest dispenser of energy 142

The meaning of the instruction "Subdue the
Earth" and of the spiritual law "Like
attracts like" 143

Ether power as nourishment instead of the
satisfaction of the lust of the palate 144

Illnesses, physical and spiritual death
as the result of wrong thinking and acting 146

Part 2:
The Spiritual Vegetarian – Self-Healing
of Various Illnesses

Structure and function of the ether body –
The soul and the physical body 149

What is a spiritual vegetarian? 152

Conduct with headaches –
Possible causes of this complaint 154

Relief of tension and pain through meditation 164

Patience and persistent devotion to God
are decisive for success 167

The human being should consciously turn to
the strengthening ether powers early
in the morning 170

The healing ether powers in dew 172

The alignment with the magnetic currents
of the Earth – A support for the sick or
weak organism 175

Beneficial effects of water veins and the
crossing of water veins 179

How can people who possess special spiritual
abilities, for instance, dowsers, be tested? 181

Healing meditation for brain tumors and mental
retardation. Pointers for the absorption of the
Earth's magnetic currents with brain injury,
epilepsy and the like 182

Invocation of the ether powers with headaches,
migraine and brain disorders 186

The surrender solely to the will of God is
necessary – Dangers involved with invoking
the Spirit power 187

Illnesses in your head can be relieved or healed
by activating the sixth consciousness center 188

Prerequisites for the effectiveness of the
healing ether powers in a person 191

The ether tree in the human being supplies all the
organs of the body with the holy ether power –
Significance of the seven consciousness centers 193

Increased activity of the ether powers by way
of self-analysis and refinement 201

Healing meditation and healing exercises 203

Directions for activating the fifth consciousness
center – Toothache, festering tonsils, illnesses
of the respiratory organs 207

Praise the cells of your body – The life force
in them will increase 211

Finishing the healing meditation –
Subsequent thoughts and actions 212

The correct use of medicines and
medicinal herbs 214

The life is in the herbs – The ether power is
the best remedy 216

The various effects of the sun's radiation 218

About the thyroid gland and its treatment 223

Get to know the anatomy of your
soul body and activate the
consciousness centers 227

Further instructions for activating the fifth
consciousness center – Larynx,
vocal cords, breathing 232

About the fourth center of consciousness 237

Further instructions for activating the fourth
center of consciousness – Heart and
circulatory problems 240

There is no illness in the domain
of the Spirit – Fear and worries open
the door wide for illness 243

Instructions for illnesses of the lungs – Rules
for a short and an extended meditation 245

Composure – An upright posture –
Physical exercises 253

The second and third consciousness centers 255

The spiritual treatment of the spinal column 259

Your digestive organ, the stomach, also obeys
the third consciousness center 262

Changing our thought and practice into a
God-conscious, positive way of thinking
and acting 269

Spheres of purification and incarnations –
Their significance for the development
of the soul 275

An operation – Turning point and opportunity
in the life of a human being 281

Your fate lies in your hand 284

Conduct before surgery 286

The first consciousness center:
Coccyx area 293

Summary of the wisdom vital for
healing body and soul 303

Daily preparation of the soul in the morning 306

How can I keep my soul and body in harmony? 309

Part 3:
Further Instructions and Recommendations
Concerning Certain Illnesses

Increased performance and equilibrium
by positively charging the magnetic field 312

Conduct when feeling fatigue, depression
and loss of energy 313

The frequencies of the ocean waves increase
the vitality of the body and the life forces
of the soul 315

Why older people like to feed birds 316

General indications for the illness of cancer 316

The healing effects of rye and wheat fields 318

The ether powers of various kinds of moss
and of forest grass 319

Cleansing the body should also take place
from within 320

Advice for scrofula and psoriasis 321

Ulcers, wounds and burns 323

Part 4:
The Various Fragrances and
Their Effects 324

Part 5:
The Significance of Colors and Sounds and
Their Effects on the Soul and the Person 327

Part 6:
To Attain Spiritual Evolution, a Life According
to the Laws of the Lord Is Necessary –
Summary of the most important laws of God-
revealed in this book 356

Every soul must complete the seven basic
levels of the Spirit 359

   Order 360

   Will 363

Wisdom 366

Earnestness 367

Patience 369

Love 370

Mercy 372

Schematic Drawing of the
Consciousness Centers 376

Latin Nomenclature of Herbs 378

Further Books 380

PREFACE

The message from the All at hand was given to humankind in the years 1980/81, via the prophetic word of Gabriele, the prophetess and emissary of God in our time. Back then, nature was still mostly healthy. For human beings, nature is a fount of health, since the physical body consists of the four elements of this Earth, called fire, water, earth and air. Thus, since the human body is a body of nature, the forces of nature are active as healing powers for the human being who opens them for himself. How this can take place in the right way, was explained to us in detailed form in this revelation. However, at this time today, (2017) much, very much, in and on the Earth has been polluted, that is, it has been thrown out of balance. This is why many statements on the effectiveness of the gifts of nature can no longer be fulfilled as originally given.

Nevertheless, this book can continue to give basic, valuable indications, particularly in view of the spiritual correlations between the thinking and acting of the human being and the health of his soul and of his physical body, and much more.

We know that this time will pass away. The Earth will cleanse itself of what the all-too-human thinking and doings have done to it. A spiritual age is dawning, with people who fulfill the laws of God more and more, who respect the life in all its forms, who are in consonance and in communication with the forces of nature on the Earth that is becoming ever brighter.

Let us take this work given by the Spirit of God as a help to orient us in our daily life – and as a prospect for the new Earth. In and on the new Earth ,it will again be as it was once, and is, intended by God, the Eternal. Nature will be healthy. Therefore, today and in a later time, we will be able to see how, via nature, God has cared for us, His children in the earthly garment.

In the Spirit, there is no time. What will be, is already present today in the Spirit. Thus, this book is a historical work already now – and also for the coming time.

August 2017

FOREWORD

In the name, and according to the will of the Lord, the almighty Spirit, the Cherub of divine Wisdom – on Earth called spiritual teacher Brother Emanuel, the responsible servant of the Lord in His Homebringing Mission – gives a revelation through the prophetess of the Lord.

This multifaceted work gives humankind a deep insight into the laws of God.

The ethereal powers, which are very often mentioned in this revelation in particular, are the law of the Spirit. The eternal law of the Lord is based on flowing, eternally spiritual-divine ether. The divine ether is a force of both healing and life. It nourishes the pure beings as well as souls and human beings, and especially those who turn to God, their Lord and Father, in Christ, their Redeemer.

This revelation should be taken very seriously. The activation and application of the divine ether powers are revealed in it. It is advisable for our brothers and sisters, the readers, to stimulate these forces only if they are willing to lead a life according to the will of God. However, the one who wants to activate these powers of the law for only a brief time, that is, only to achieve a successful healing, is advised not to do so.

May every person who does not open up these powers of the law with God and under His guidance – perhaps doing it only carelessly – be told that sooner or later, he will have to suffer very much for this. Thus, the one who causes these powers to flow more strongly by using techniques and practices and without leading a lawful life will feel the abuse of these powers in a very painful manner, either in this life or a future one.

This revelation is given to willing God-seekers as a gift, toward gaining spiritual recognition and maturity.

May it be said to all curious people who merely want to try out this revealed knowledge: Do not sin against the law of the Lord, for every action is followed by a corresponding reaction! Neither the divine world, which revealed these deep truths, nor the publishers of this revelation, are liable for any mental, spiritual or physical damage. This work is recommended only for the one who earnestly turns to God and wants to change his life by actualizing the laws of the Lord.

The purposeful address of the spiritual ether powers and the manner of healing connected with this are taught in the second meditation course of Universal Life. Through deep meditation, a close spiritual-mental connection is made with the ether power, the Holy Spirit, and with every physical organ.

The divine world desires that all brothers and sisters seriously change their life and make use of these inner powers of God.

Some fundamental truths will be repeated in this revelation. This is because the human being has to build on these basic principles of life, in order to reach his goal in life. These repetitions of the spiritual laws are necessary so that the individual explanations are always seen in the right perspective and do not become independent of each other. In this way, each willing person is able to grasp and understand the details.

The repetitions make for better understanding by helping the reader as well as the one seeking healing to understand better, when wanting to actualize what is revealed through a corresponding way of life.

PART 1

The Human Being as an Energy Field of the Spirit – The Right Way of Life to Stay Healthy and Spiritually Active

*The positive or negative programming
in the morning is decisive*

The human being is a vibrating body of energy. Thousands of rays hit this body every minute, which may either keep it healthy or harm it. It all depends on the person's behavior in his everyday life, and especially, on how he programs himself in the morning, shortly after awakening.

We can imagine every human being as a planet that irradiates its surrounding planets, that is, other people, with potentially high powers. In the morning, the planet "human being" enters its orbit. What is decisive is the orbit he chooses. As soon as he awakens and his senses become active, thousands of rays penetrate him more intensely, because the world of his sensations immediately attracts them. An unknowing person allows these rays to direct him at will. A knowing person makes use of these cosmic influences by sorting them out immediately upon awakening and by programming certain rays that will then lead and guide him throughout the day, according to his programming.

I will begin with a person who leaves the promising rays of life or the penetrating negative radiation to chance.

The unknowing person, who identifies solely with this world, wakes up in the morning feeling lethargic and listless. His joy in life is mostly limited to material things. Everything else, the purely divine and spiritual, is beyond his thoughts and actions. Such a person provides a vessel into which all kinds of different rays flow. Already in the morning when he awakens, he first becomes aware of his own aura and of the people around him, the momentary impressions, the time of day and his physical well-being. A worldly person is immediately preoccupied with himself and with the approaching matters and events of the day. At the very moment that he preoccupies himself with his past, present, or future problems, he sets free a bundle of forces that have not yet fully affected him.

These are mostly energies that already surround him and are merely waiting to be called up in order to become active. These are, in part, vibrations that are already in the aura of the worldly person and are brought into higher vibration by his thinking about them. But often, the externally oriented person attracts not only the aspects that are found in his own aura, but also the vibrations of other people whom he thinks of in the morning, and whose problems are connected with his own. In this way, he already programs himself for the dawning day, but often, also for days and weeks. The world is saturated with more negative than positive rays. They are just waiting to influence a person and to lead him.

Positive rays, as well, are waiting to be called upon, in order to become effective. These rays, however, are harmonizing and upbuilding. These high frequencies can be called up and used only by people with a high spiritual vibration.

Especially in the morning, between four and seven o'clock, these spiritual rays are very active and want to help, soothe and heal. These rays, also called odic forces, build up between 10:00 PM and 4:00 AM, when the human senses are resting. These odic forces, also called odic rays, are also active during the day. However, they do not become fully effective in the person, since his five senses are totally oriented to without in an uncontrolled way. In many cases, these odic forces cannot prove useful for a person because he does not include them in his life. For this reason, they adhere to trees, flowers and shrubs in increased measure. Most of all, they cling to coniferous trees, because these, being more highly developed, have a stronger magnetic charge.

This is why regions rich in woodlands have a higher ozone concentration, which, insofar as it is absorbed through the power of thoughts or with proper breathing, can be a fount of health for body and soul. Therefore, a spiritually knowing person already makes use of these healing powers early in the morning. On the other hand, the worldly person blocks these helpful spiritual ether powers, because his thoughts are connected solely with the world.

We have to imagine every solar system in infinity as a battery that during certain cycles is connected to a high source of energy. Consequently, the Earth also receives an increased amount of the life energies that come from the primordial power. When a continent has turned away from the sun and people come to rest, these ether powers become fully effective. The inflow of spiritual energies is continuous. However, they cannot always become effective, because the planet "human being," who does not align with them in his thoughts, words and actions, is unable to accept them. Every radiation consists of certain kinds of spiritual atoms, which, of themselves, are perfect. Some of these high, purely cosmic powers are transformed down through humankind's unlawful behavior.

Within and without his body, a person can address both the positive spiritual powers, as well as the negative worldly powers. In this way, he brings certain kinds of atoms into vibration. These vibrations either penetrate the inner being of a person via his aura or they are already in his disposition and trigger the corresponding resonances in his inner being. Unlawful vibrations burden a person. Positive ones stimulate him and give peace and health to the person who has a positive attitude.

Just *one* thought, no matter what vibration it has, can trigger a chain of positive or negative forces that will soon affect the person, influencing and controlling his disposition and his whole body. Even thoughts that were already dismissed by a person, but are still quiescent in his aura and being dissolved by the ether powers, can still be called back by the originator and become active again. Things that were forgotten long ago, which already may even be in the ether chronicle and are being dissolved there, can be called up and brought into action again at the last minute through the power of a person's thoughts. In this way, things often appear again in the image of humankind that had long been part of the past. This can be brought about by the thought-power of just one person alone. Long past quarrels, feelings of hatred, unrest and even illnesses and the like can be brought back again by the power of thought. Such unlawful thought-actions can then begin to move in people who think negatively, or in countries with a very negative aura, bringing with it grievous consequences. Everything is controlled by the power of thoughts, since everything is based on vibration.

An unknowing person who has completely oriented himself to the material life will also think, act and live according to his surroundings. The worldly person enjoys a long night's sleep and lets himself drift on the ocean of this world during the day – merely as a result of having programmed himself in a worldly way in the morning. Only when his blows of fate catch up with him will he, perhaps, begin to think about things, or he will rail against his God and reach for the nearest bottle of pills.

If the hours of the morning are used as intended by the divine and a corresponding morning programming takes place, this is the best medicine. The cosmic forces are high sources of energy and can be absorbed especially well during the morning hours, when the body is still in harmony. They flow from God's pharmacy, and are the water of life for every cell of the body. You, O human being, may receive them!

The proper use of this valuable remedy is found in a correct attitude toward the spiritual-divine life. Your first thought in the morning will either open or close your soul and person for this life force. Your first thought, and thus, your alignment with the existing life forces that are waiting to be called on, is essential.

Many people wake up in a grumpy mood. They either did not sleep well, or they were plagued by dreams during the night that reflect their life. Physical complaints may appear here and there, which already cause their day to start badly. Disruptive thoughts, at night as well as during the day, are nothing other than the result of negative programming on a daily basis. The person who is preoccupied only with material things is no longer able to leave the forest of his thoughts. Whatever moves him or causes him pain in the morning, he takes with him into the day and into his sleep at night. Through this wrong way of living, he is constantly surrounded by his self-created world of vibrations. These vibrations that developed in him also cause resonances in the sphere of his external life, in the world.

Such a negatively polarized person not only lets his vibrations created by him run free, but at the same time he awakens these vibrations in his neighbor who is on the same vibrational level, or he projects them into the atmosphere, from where they will certainly hit him again. With an uncontrolled way of living, a person remains in the energy field of unlawful forces, which harm his nerves and cells more and more. These constantly unlawful resonances weaken the body and lead to illness. Sooner or later – perhaps not until a future life – these human ways of thinking and acting will show their effects. These unlawful ways also lead to aggressions and excesses that damage the soul. These constant offences create the envelopments of the soul. A soul may go through several incarnations until these soul-garments come loose and the physical body feels the burden of the soul.

From these explanations, a person can see how decisive the first thoughts upon awakening are. Therefore, examine and monitor yourself each day. Practice thinking and acting in the right way, then your soul and your body will not suffer harm. High and noble thoughts are upbuilding ether powers, which keep you healthy and strong throughout your whole life on Earth. These ether powers are the best remedy.

Your body is not only dependent on proper nutrition – as many people think – but above all, on positive, upbuilding ethereal thoughts. Every cell of your body is a child that wants to be treated lovingly, so that it can react and live accordingly. Therefore, give your cells, your body's children, positive thoughts. They will reward you, during the night as well as the day, because they vibrate in the rhythm of the high ether power.

A positive programming in the morning helps the ether powers to unfold in you. As soon as a person has acquired a divine, that is, a lawful, life rhythm, his eating habits also change. The body reacts more to the harmonious ether powers than to the forces of the world, which crave the unlawful, unsettle a person and pull him down into the depths of baseness.

Program yourself in the morning in such a way that you first say a prayer. However, it must be spoken out of conviction that a higher power exists, which lives and is active in you, in your own soul. This inner power is the divine ether, the spark of the soul, which carries all cosmic, upbuilding powers for a harmonious life. When you pray, then think of the One who should hear your prayer. Know that every thought can bring you sorrow or joy. Therefore, pray to God, your Lord, from the depths of your heart, so that He may become your guide in daily life. God is your Father. He, the Lord, wants to provide His child solely with love and goodness. God, your Father, is above worldly things. He, the Lord, knows and beholds everything. Your Father knows the condition of your soul. He sees the dangers that are lurking around you. He, the Lord, your Father, keeps track of your eternal life. The Lord alone can guide you, protect you and keep you healthy. He, your Father, is the greatest power in infinity. What do you fear then, since God, the Spirit, your Father, lives in you?

Fear yourself, O human being, your own base thoughts and deeds. The thought-powers, which you have called forth yourself, bring you weal or woe. Therefore, if you are the cause of your suffering, then see the enemy in yourself. Your present way of thinking, living and acting determines your future. It can become a curse or a blessing for you. No one can harm you if you are in absolute harmony with the highest power in you, with your heavenly Father. Your own godless thoughts release forces and attract base, unlawful forces that can bring you more harm than benefit. Therefore, know, O human being, that upon awakening, a heart-prayer awakens the holy powers slumbering in you, and that they will influence you positively throughout the entire day, if you include them in your life again and again during the day.

The Spirit of your eternal Father is in every cell of your body, and also in every cell of your neighbor. If a person can activate these holy powers, he creates an aura that is indestructible, that will protect him from all negative influences, from illnesses and negative worldly powers – provided this is good for his life, and, above all, for his soul.

If you have now prayed and linked with God, your Father, whose Spirit dwells in the inner part of your soul, then program your brain cells. Speak to this legion of cells and align them with the positive, high vibrations of the Spirit.

Speak to them as follows, analogously:

"I now speak to the cells of my body." Begin with the brain cells. Speak with them and mean what you are saying. A lukewarm attempt without any emphasis of good will behind it does not reach the legion of cells. Remember, O human being, the power of the Absolute, the power of the law, is in every cell. Today, you want to think solely in accordance with this power. God, the Lord, said: "You, therefore, must be perfect as your heavenly Father is perfect." This statement, O human being, should be your guideline. No negative thoughts should find a place in your brain cells. Resist all aggressions, no matter where they may come from, and program your legion of cells with the sentence: "I am the stillness." Protect yourself from all excitement and hectic activity, no matter where it may come from, whether from people or technology.

Think over and over again: "There is nothing that I am afraid of, because the Spirit of God is in each and every cell of my body. I place myself under His almighty guidance."

Say to your heart, to your circulatory system and to all other cells and organs:
"May every cell come into harmony and remain in harmony with the Infinite.
No pathogens can affect me because the Infinite is effective in every cell of my body. I command my stomach to crave only healthy nourishment and to orient itself accordingly.
I command my palate to stir only when the organism really needs food, and to then want only foods that are in accordance with the law.
May my hormones and glands be active according to the rhythm indicated by the Infinite in me, and not react to external influences.
I remain in harmony during the whole day.
I do not absorb anything offensive.
The Lord in me shall be my guide.

May the Absoluteness consciously go with me my whole life long, and make me aware of all still existing faults, until my heart rests fully in God, my Father."

The one who surrounds himself with these high thought-powers every morning, and reminds himself of them again and again during the day, by making contact with the Infinite through a brief, but sincere, prayer of thanksgiving, will be a spiritually knowing person who consciously makes the hours between four and seven o'clock in the morning a part of his day. The inner and outer powers serve such a person.

The spiritually knowing, positively attuned person

What happens when the human being goes to the divine power in the morning?

First of all, he awakens the spiritual powers that are in him, and secondly, he also attracts the odic forces that built up during the night. These powers flow to him from nature's sphere of life. They strengthen his organism and provide him with additional protection. The primordial power in the innermost part of the soul as well as the odic forces of nature are ready to serve the human being. The inner power links with the forces of nature and creates a spiritual aura, a protective shell for a positively programmed person. The negative forces are kept away by the high gifts of the Spirit, through which the entire cell structure of the body attains a higher vibration.

With such a positive attitude, a person comes into harmony with the Infinite, enabling him to economize with his energies in such a way that he needs only a few hours of sleep. By this economizing with the powers of the Spirit, the entire cell structure of the body attains a high divine vibration over the course of time. Thus, in only a few hours of the night the body can regain the strength that it gave off in a lawful way during the day.

As long as a person cannot yet totally restrain his thoughts and his human temperament gets the better of him every now and then, he should program himself several times during the day, perhaps during the morning, if possible, shortly before lunchtime, so that he partake of foods that only benefit his body and do not overtax his organism.

If a person is very restless and externally oriented, then a programming in the evening would also be advisable. This should take place early in the evening or shortly before going to bed. The person should again speak to his cells. Whenever you speak to your body cells, you are simultaneously speaking to your soul, because both the cells of the body and the soul react to sensations, thoughts, words and actions. O human being, explain to your cell state that silence is holy and that you wish it a restoring sleep. Praise your cell state and your organs, as well. The whole organism will thank you.

Pray to God, your Father, whose Spirit dwells in your soul and in every cell of your body, and thank Him, most of all, for His daily help and protection. Ask your Father, whose Spirit dwells in you, for further powers that build up the soul, so that you may daily draw closer to Him, the Lord of life.

Do not think solely of your physical body, but above all, of your soul body, for a healthy soul also has a healthy body.

Your soul matures in the following way: If a person asks the Infinite, the Father, to build up his soul, the soul's powers will increase especially during the night. The core of being in the innermost part of the soul, which consists of two active light-forces (the positive and negative particles), comes into movement with the prayer-invocation, through which it increasingly attracts ether powers from the purely spiritual spheres of creation. Via the two particles, via the core of being, these energetic powers then flow into the particles of the soul and try to purify them from the burdens of this world. Through this energetic release of powers, a karma in the soul can be dissolved. If it is a minor soul-burden, it may flow out in dreams while sleeping. It is possible that the soul may take parts of these dreams into its conscious state, when awake. Therefore, a true God-seeker should not worry about unpleasant and upsetting dreams. It can be that a cleansing of the soul takes place in this way.

However, a severe karma, a severe soul-burden, can also be released through this energetic thrust. You may awaken feeling indisposed and sick in the morning. A God-seeker who already has spiritual knowledge will think about it and will not bring the cells of his body into turmoil by reacting with grouchiness, thus influencing his awakening cell state with base thoughts that make it passive. Pray to God, your Father. Be thankful for everything, regardless of what happened to your body during the night. It is not the Spirit of love that sent you this outflowing soul-burden. You inflicted this karma on yourself, in this or in former lives. Speak to your legion of cells, and, with encouraging thoughts or words, stimulate it to resist. By repeatedly addressing your cells with encouraging words, you promote the powers of resistance in your body, which are the policemen of the body. If it is the will of the Lord, they will deploy in your body and fight the illness.

Jesus once spoke in the following sense: "Go forth and sin no more!" With this, the Lord meant the sinfulness in thoughts, words and deeds. Always think positive and constructive thoughts. Then, the good and divine will serve you. It is said that if a person believes in God and keeps His commandments, he is under the flow of the Holy Spirit. Every karma can be relieved or healed through the Holy Spirit of the inner being.

If the core of being of the soul was active during the night and a karma was released from the soul into the body, then the legion of your cells and the policemen of your body become active immediately, if you speak to them encouragingly, because the Spirit of God is active in every cell of your body.

If the child of God, the person, does not react querulously, but speaks lovingly to his cell state, inspired by the deep knowledge that the Spirit of God is in every cell, he simultaneously addresses the Spirit powers in his cells. As a result, the following correlations can become effective: Because of the encouraging conversation with the cells of the body, these – triggered by the positive thoughts – attract active odic forces that built up during the night. Thus, not only the inner healing powers will take effect, but also the odic forces that are flowing in from without. These ethereal powers have a stimulating and upbuilding effect via the aura of the person. According to their rate of vibration, the active cells of the body attract these ether powers. They then help to defend against pathogens that have penetrated the body.

Everything is based on vibration. The fine-material, as well as the coarse-material universe, consists of vibration. If the cell children need the corresponding odic forces of evergreen trees or meadows to defend against pathogens – depending on the type of bacteria or virus – these odic vibrations are attracted by the cell state and supplied to the sick body cells. If a person is able to trustingly and totally surrender to his God and Father, the combined activity of the inner forces with the external odic forces can lead to a significantly faster healing effect.

All of creation, the spiritual as well as the material, vibrates and pulsates. Every little herb, all existing life forms, are surrounded by a spiritual aura, by odic forces, which are also called ether powers. A person on the path to God, whose goal is the Lord, can call up these powers, insofar as he keeps the laws of the Lord.

If the cell state is in need of the upbuilding powers of herbs, for example, of dandelions or ribwort plantain*, simply through the power of his thoughts a light-filled person can call up the odic forces that vibrate around this plant. The magnetic soul attracts these odic forces. The positively influenced cell children thankfully accept the odic forces of the plants and, with this odic vibration, influence their cell brothers and sisters that have been weakened by illness.

If a person has turned within and allows his divine Father to prevail as the guide and leader in his life, then even his glands and hormones can absorb

---

* Note: Since many of the names for herbs vary from region to region and country to country, please refer to the Index Key at the end of this book for the Latin nomenclature.

the strengthening particles of the moon. A few days before a full moon, the rays of the moon, in particular, are very active.

During this time, a very high emission of moon particles takes place. Glands and hormones react to these highly vibrating forces, which can also be attracted by the power of thoughts of a person with a positive attitude.

If a person constantly lives in the divine communication, there is a constant interaction between him and the Inner Physician, the Spirit of God. Through this spiritual connection, the person is able to live in constant harmony with the external positive forces. Over the course of time, your body will no longer need earthly medicine, because the Spirit of your Father is fully effective in all the cells, glands and hormones. If you are in harmony with the divine, the Inner Physician can be at your side, ready to help. You, O human being, can depend on the Inner Physician. He, the Lord, whose Spirit lives in you, is all-knowing and, thus, also knows about you. The dose that the Inner Physician determines for you is the most precise one. It serves your well-being. Do not complain or accuse your cell children. This will only make them tired and listless.

Recognize yourself as your greatest enemy. By being unknowing, by sending out ignoble sensations and thoughts and by unlawful actions, you have damaged your legion of cells. Repent of your faults and weaknesses and do not sin henceforth, neither in feelings and thoughts, nor in words or deeds. Then you will come into harmony with the Infinite, with God, your Father, with the Inner Physician and Healer.

The Spirit, who is in all things, wants to especially serve His most beautiful creatures, His children. All of creation bows before the most beautiful creatures, the children of God. The mineral, plant and animal kingdoms want to serve the great light, the child of God. Only when your light has become greater than that of all these kingdoms will you be in constant harmony with God and His life forms. This will enable you to address the odic forces as well as the inner forces in a lawful way and to pass them on to your fellowman.

*The law and impact of the holy,
divine ether powers*

The ether power is the eternally existing Spirit power. Its starting point is the two primordial forces of creation, the two particles. All of creation emerged from these two particles, called plus and minus or positive and negative. The ether is the spirit-substance and the bearer of all life. In all existing forms of being, the two primordial forces form the core of life, the core of being. These two particles are the most powerful ether powers. All of creation breathes through their power of love. Without these two particles, there would be no life. They form the foundation of the whole, the foundation of all spiritual and material worlds. They are the core of being, the outpouring power in all spiritual atoms, which are the building blocks of all life.

These two particles brought forth the eternal creation of the Being. From them, emerged the ether powers, which were still flowing in uncontrolled orbits. They were put in order by the two primordial powers. In this way, the spiritual atoms developed, that is, the various ether or energy streams, which precisely arranged themselves around the core of being that orders and maintains everything.

In every fruit is the seed or seeds that bear the life. Every seed contains its respective species. I am thinking of an apple or a plum or any other kind of fruit. The germ bud bears the absolute power for each species. The flesh does not produce the new life, but the core, the seed, does.

This is why, according to the laws of the spiritual kingdom, the divine core of life, which is the primordial force in every spiritual atom, has to be addressed if the basic powers in the person are to unfold. The divine elements answer only if the core of being is addressed. The law of God, and thus, its forces, can be recognized and experienced only when the person concerned practices love, for the core of being is love, the greatest power in the universe.

To master the elements so that they serve each individual and the totality, the love for all existing divine life forms has to be actualized, since love is the basic thought, the basic power in creation. In order to subdue the heavens and the Earth in the right way, each created being must have the right kind of love for all of creation and, above all, for God, its Creator. Therefore, whoever wants to master the elements and to subdue all of life must live the immutable law, the love, and at that, the love for all people, souls, beings and life forms. The life forms are the mineral, plant and animal kingdoms. However, most of all, he must love his heavenly Father above all things, who is the core of life of all Being.

Therefore, there is need to recognize that everything that exists has its origin in creation, and that the Creator, our Lord and God, who gives the power to master the elements, answers His child only if the child of God turns to Him, the core of being of life, and acknowledges Him. Only then, will the elements obey the person.

What would a person have to do to be able to master them? What is essential and everlasting is *the* commandment, or the law, the love. Without love for the entire creation and, above all, for the Creator-God, nothing is possible and thus, nothing is lasting. The person who does not live in harmony with the divine elements, and thus, with the Infinite, with his Father, will destroy himself and his environment. Whatever he created has no lasting permanence. Even while it is being created, it is already subject to decay and destruction. This is why the matter that was created by the Fall-beings cannot exist in eternity, because the Creator-God and the eternal kingdom are fine-material. This means that the Spirit is flowing ether and the pure spirit beings that remained in the Spirit of God are likewise fine-material, weightless, light and absolutely ethereal, we could say, fully active in their radiation, since in the kingdom of life everything is based on the pure ether power.

A human being's soul, like the ethereal body of the pure spirit beings, is the bearer of all components of the universe. Therefore, second to God, its Father, the soul possesses the highest spiritual powers. The child of God is the highest and most beautiful creature in the universe. It unites all spiritual-energetic forces in itself.

In all ethereal and pure spirit beings, every spiritual atom is fully formed and active. The soul of a human being is a spirit being of heaven, only incarnated and burdened with unlawful aspects. This is why the ether body is called soul, because it surrounded itself with the garments of its fate, causing the ether body, the soul, to become unknowing and humanized. The spirit-body became more and more veiled through this envelopment of the soul, that is, through the unlawful thinking and acting of the spirit being, which initiated the Fall toward condensation. Finally, it became a diminished structure, which had enveloped itself with its self-created, unlawful aspects. This coarse-material shell is what we call the physical body.

To activate the Spirit power, the ether power, the human being must let the Spirit become effective in him, by surrendering authority to the Spirit. Only when the Spirit in the person, the core of being, prevails over matter, will the person experience the illumination of his body, through which he can gradually become a God-person. The elements obey such a person, because through a lawful life, he is able to address every element, that is, every spiritual atom.

As long as humankind violates the eternally existing law in thoughts and deeds, its self-inflicted fate will catch up with it again and again. Because of humankind's negative actions, it cannot rise above its yoke. Thus, it moves deeper and deeper into material decline. Humankind lives with its technical innovations and believes to be educated and knowledgeable. It boasts about its achievements and believes to have achieved much during the past centuries.

Compared to the ether powers, which everyone has in himself and which everyone could apply by living in accordance with the laws of God, the present human civilization, in comparison, rather equals the achievements of Stone Age man. How a person of the Spirit could live and what he could accomplish is still unknown to humankind. The individual must work hard for his own livelihood and that of a whole nation.

The Lord said: "Pray and work." But in wise foresight, He also said: "You shall earn your bread by the sweat of your brow." This means that if you do not apply the ether powers, you will have to work hard, very hard. However, the one who can pray in the right way and aligns his life to the divine will be increasingly served by the ether powers – provided his soul has been sufficiently purified.

Several times already, the Spirit of truth has spoken of people who move huge amounts of earth and build noisy machines. Even if they think that their technology is not loud, this is merely a false conclusion, for they know little about the calm, peacefully vibrating powers of the Spirit. Every level of noise, even the words of people, disturbs the cosmic harmony and prevents the coarse-material structure, matter, from refining.

This is also true for human beings. Much uncontrolled speaking and gesticulating disturb the soul and lead to tension in the soul and in the cell structure of the body. The ether powers, the eternally existing law, and the ether forms of the Spirit are gently flowing, noiseless forces. None of the pure spirit beings gesticulate as human beings do; nor do they utter such disharmonious sounds. The eternal beings have the language of light. This means that they express themselves by way of sensations. This is why there is eternal stillness in the eternal Being. No disharmonious sound disturbs the cosmic activity and the continually flowing, harmonious ether powers. All four existing elements are harmoniously attuned to each other and bring forth everlasting colors and lawful forms.

The noisier and louder the behavior of humankind is and the higher the noise level it creates, the more it represses the holy ether powers, which react to the negative vibrations of all noises and either withdraw or remain latent. However, no vibration that has been sent out is lost. The positive as well as the negative vibrations find their echo. The positively emitted streams link with the divine ether powers. The negative vibrations remain in the atmosphere, paralyze the Spirit power and fall back on their originators, taking on form more and more.

The willfulness of the fallen spirit beings led to the condensation of matter, to the human being with his illnesses and blows of fate

These unlawful forces had already contributed to the formation of matter. They reduced the high spiritual ether powers, rendering them largely ineffective and keeping them latent. The highest condensation of the ether – matter – developed through the billions of years of unlawful activity of the fallen spirit beings. The willfulness of the fallen spirit beings, which became more and more condensed, created time and space. The Spirit of God respects the free will of His children. With the recognition of the self-created causes, remorse sets in, whereupon the divine life can then build itself up again.

I already mentioned several times that everything is based on vibration. As long as humankind does not align with the eternally existing law of God, it will be unable to free itself from its plagues, illnesses and blows of fate. Even when the human being tries desperately to combat illness by examining and analyzing pathogens in laboratories to find remedies, all this is mere delusion.

In this context, a parable: Let us think of a porous water hose that leaks in several places. A person tries to patch these damaged spots. But this is merely an ostensible success. Sooner or later this porous water hose will leak again, usually in another spot.

Over the course of billions of years, the fine-material body of the fallen spirit beings became more and more encapsulated, that is to say, it condensed more and more, thus transforming itself down to the human being. The cells and organs, the entire human body, are condensed fields of vibration, wrongly polarized spiritual atoms, which gradually took on the envelopment of the material form.

Therefore, when the human being has found a new remedy for this or that illness in his laboratories, he merely patches one organ in the sick body. The illness, however, often breaks out again in another cell structure. It may appear with quite different symptoms. Again, there are remedies for this; again, another patch, until this illness, which may have been a soul-burden that was flowing out into the body, is pushed back into the soul, into the soul body. This makes the soul body insensitive again for the spiritual, because an unlawful patch, the earthly medicine, does not allow the all-knowing, wise and healing ether power to become active.

The person who merely appears to be healed believes that he has done everything for his body, because he became healthy – as it momentarily seems. The doctor is glad and the scientists are proud of themselves, because they believe they have found an effective medicine that fights against the causes of the illness. But it was merely a patch on an already very porous hose.

This is also how all of humankind treats its Earth. The noises and detonations form the holes in the porous hose, the Earth; prayer-thoughts from good people who live in God put patches on them. However, with its unlawful way of living, the majority of humankind is in the process of constantly surrounding the Earth and itself with base vibrations. This causes the porous Earth – seen symbolically as a hose – to break open in other places. And then, the human being speaks of natural disasters or of divine retribution. In reality, *he* is the one who created the causes and advanced the effects.

Only with the ennoblement of humankind, of every single person, could the Earth and the whole solar system regain health. Only once humankind regains health from within, from the soul, from the core of being, which is in every soul and in every human being, can the dwelling-planet Earth also be raised through a refined vibration, which would have to come from human beings. In this way, it would be brought into higher vibration, allowing for human beings and the solar system to be integrated into a lawful rhythm, and the regression of the coarse-material into the fine-material could take a lawful course. With this refinement, the person's illnesses and blows of fate, as well as natural disasters, would decrease, because the eternally existing ether powers, the iron law of God, could refine the coarse-material with increased intensity.

*Lawful thoughts and actions
lead back into the energy field
of the divine Spirit*

What would a person have to do to change his life and to be able to address the elements? The good as well as the bad go out from the person and his burdened soul. This unlawfulness caused disharmony in a part of creation. It is the fallen spirit beings, which, through their thoughts and actions, enveloped themselves with self-created powers and gradually became the rigid form of the human being. The disembodied soul takes with it the malice and unknowingness, which arose from the human ego, into the realms of purification. From there, it influences those human beings who have a similar vibration and are therefore receptive for its insinuations. Through this, the Earth remains the field of operation for such souls. As human beings, they did not purify their senses and took the same line as many of our unknowing and obstinate, incarnated brothers and sisters.

Several times over the course of a human being's lifetime, the Spirit gives him the chance to recognize his present life and to change it. However, the lazy human being seldom perceives the indications of his own fate, because this would mean that he would have to turn back and make an effort. Thus, he would have to purify himself before giving good advice to his fellowman.

Through a lawful way of thinking and acting on the part of every single human being, the environment and the Earth would also be put right and serve humankind. As a result, the souls in the spheres of purification would also have to think better of it, since the object of their influence, the human being, would no longer listen to their negative insinuations.

What could happen if all of humankind were to change and strive toward what is good and lawful? First, the human being would purify himself from all base drives. Through this, his soul would come into an ever higher vibration. The power that makes this possible is the Spirit power, the ether, which permeates the purified soul more and more. With the devotion to the good and lawful, the eternally existing ether power could gradually gain control over the people. Through this increased power-potential, the person would become more and more imbued with light. This means that his basic attitude toward his neighbor would be good and could contribute to a further ascent. A lawful way of life would bring people closer and closer together and they would become true brothers. In time, there would no longer be any country borders, since the eternal Spirit, the ether power, could become effective as the prevailing consciousness in the people. As soon as the Spirit gains control of an individual, the person changes from within, that is, from the core of being of his soul. This takes place as follows:

As soon as a person recognizes an indication of his own fate, which is a pointer from God, and consequently changes for the better, the core of being in the soul begins to pulsate more intensely.

The Spirit gently draws the person's attention to his errors and weaknesses. The Spirit of God and the guardian spirit work closely together in this effort. Preparing a person for the good starts by way of the conscience. In the cerebrum, right under the skull, there are many highly sensitive cell membranes that vibrate much more easily and rapidly than the other brain cells. These cells form the conscience. They are touched first by the Spirit of God, the core of being, and the guardian spirit, through which they become the policemen of the person, as it were. As soon as the person wants to turn to the good and the Absolute, the polarity of these cells reverses, which means they are oriented toward the flowing ether power. In this way, it is possible for the Spirit of God to make a person aware of his unlawful aspects time and again.

With the already mentioned devotion to the good, the core of being in the soul, the primordial power, which had been largely latent thus far, becomes active. First of all, it attracts increased ether powers from infinity at night, while the person is asleep. Ether powers are the powers of the Spirit or of God. These powers of God then flow into the soul and, by way of the consciousness centers in soul and body, spread out in the human being.

If the person now listens to his conscience and obeys the good, the inflow of the ether powers will increase. If the good will becomes the deed, by the person sending out positive forces through thoughts, then through deeds, these brain cells, the conscience, come into an even higher vibration, for everything that vibrates causes resonance. Here is an example:

If you throw a stone into the water, you trigger vibrations in the water that, in turn, spread out in further circles. The same happens when increased Spirit power flows into a person through a life devoted to what is good and lawful. As soon as the cells of the conscience have the corresponding vibration, this vibration is transferred to the deeper-lying cell layers, mainly those of the cerebrum, through the continuous inflow of Spirit power. Once a part of the brain mass has been purified in this way, the person has left its first major efforts behind. Through this holy pushing power, the person has already undergone a partial reversal of poles toward the good, and responds more readily to the inflowing ether power, and to the admonishing voice of his guardian spirit. If the person remains on this lawful path of life, he will become a spiritual person who is more and more inclined toward the good.

So who is the triggering factor in this context? The human being! He must first turn to the ether powers, to the law of God, and do as advised. Only once the person asks for persistence in his efforts for the good and actualizes the spiritual laws that also hold true for the mineral, plant and animal kingdoms, will he consistently receive increasing amounts of spiritual power. Through these increased divine gifts, the mass of the soul expands, which then gradually covers the head and the upper half of the face. The result is that the consciousness centers in the person also expand. This starts with the lowest center, the consciousness center of Order, which is anchored in the coccyx region.

The more the person devotes himself to God during the course of this reversal of polarity, the more Spirit power flows into his soul and into his brain cells. If the resonance from these processes in the soul and in the brain cells is gradually transferred to the entire cell structure of the person, all Being will thus pulsate and vibrate. This means that through the control center, the brain, which reacts to the high energies of the Spirit, little by little, the entire body comes into the spiritual-divine vibration. The brain cells, which control the human body, signal to all the organs only what is positive, that is, good. As a result, during the course of the human life, all cells and organs of the body will react.

The law is fulfilled then, and the Spirit of God has mastery over matter, over the person. Consequently, the consciousness centers in the human body change, and gradually dissolve at the end of this spiritual process. They are replaced by higher spiritual powers that are also powers of consciousness and were thus far active only in the soul.

They are the highest ether powers, which no longer appear as wheels of consciousness but as flowing energies, which radiate more and more intensely into the expanding soul and into the body as highly potentiated ether powers. These highly potentiated ether powers form a kind of white ether flame near the coccyx region, which flickers along the spinal column and unites with the core of being in the soul.

*The unfoldment of the "God-man"
via the purification of the soul
and the expansion of the ether body*

I want to give a more detailed breakdown of the processes outlined above, which give rise to the "God-man":

The structure of the ether body is completely different from the anatomy of the physical body. The ether body has seven power centers, which are prism powers that refract into its spectrums the white light that flows out from the primordial power in the soul, the core of being. These spectral powers are the life paths of the ether body, which are in absolute harmony with the powers of the heavenly planes. This means that the spirit body, provided it is absolutely pure, is one with the entire creation. This, in turn, means that the ether body has the same makeup as the whole universe. This microcosm reacts as the macrocosm, as the entire creation. Every light path and every ether power of the universe is also fully active in the microcosm, in the pure spirit body, and can be brought into higher activity by way of the core of being and the corresponding prism powers.

The wheels of consciousness in the human body are nothing other than the seven garments with which the soul has enclosed itself through an unlawful way of life. The first four garments are the spheres of purification; the following three are the planes of preparation. The particles of the soul, too, bear the burden of these seven garments, for the soul is the book of life. Only once these garments gradually dissolve, will the particles of the soul be purified as well. Through this, the soul expands, since it receives increased Spirit powers as a result of purification. If the soul is incarnated, these seven garments of the soul form the wheels of consciousness in the human being. They gradually develop in the newborn, and begin their function unnoticed by the human being.

Thus, as soon as the soul purifies itself, this ether body expands and begins to cover the head of the person more and more. The more intensely the soul is purified, the more the divine consciousness expands as well. These highly potentiated ether powers, also called prism powers, become increasingly effective. The existing garments, which formed the wheels of consciousness in the human body, dissolve to the same extent that the soul expands and covers the person from above, from the head. These seven consciousness centers in the person become more and more light-filled through the intensified Spirit powers.

At first, the consciousness center in the area of the coccyx dissolves completely. It is replaced by the first prism-stream that gradually develops into a flame, since the soul mass expands more and more as well. These prism powers are centers of light in the ether body, in the soul. Once the soul first spreads over the upper half of the face, then over the whole face, and subsequently over the neck, the chest, and finally the whole human being, it is, nevertheless, only the physical body that is visible to the human eye, since the soul is ether. These processes, however, which take place both outside and inside the human body, can be very clearly perceived by the developing "God-man." Through this process of the reversion of polarity and of spreading over the body, the person is flooded by the divine ether power more and more strongly. The more the soul expands, the more the prism powers come into action. The consciousness centers, the garments of the soul, dissolve bit by bit, through which a completely changed flow becomes apparent in and on the person.

As long as the wheels of consciousness were active, the maturing person perceived the flowing energy of the Spirit in his body. He felt how the Spirit power flowed down, how the wheels of consciousness rotated, and how the Spirit power flowed back to the core of being. Here and there, he also perceived the Spirit powers in his organs and later, even the gentle blowing of the Holy Spirit in his body.

But as soon as the soul expands and the spirit-body emerges, the developing "God-man" notices other processes, namely, the streaming of the Spirit as expanded energy pathways, and an upward-flickering of the flame.

I had to reveal these processes in more detail, because, as mentioned, they make the human being into the "God-man." He has learned to control himself, the elements within his body, as well as the elements in the cosmos.

These processes are the metamorphosis from human being to "God-man." The changes are not visible to those who are outside of him, but are tangible to the person directly involved. All the Spirit powers of the mineral, plant and animal kingdoms serve that human being whose body obeys him, because he has fully unfolded his soul, and the elements, fire, water, earth and air, obey him. These processes, as described above, are a very slow process, which can be clearly observed by the person who walks the path of the absolute surrender of self and devotion to the Godhead. The forces serve him and the elements obey him.

*Blessedness and well-being
by the power of thoughts*

The life of God is eternally existing power.

This power originates from the spiritual atoms, which immediately become active once the human being obeys the will of God. The will of God is the driving element. The Will of the Absolute, which is also active as a power of consciousness in the human being, constantly endeavors to direct a person so that he may think high thoughts and act accordingly.

Provided the person dedicate himself to this divine schooling of his will and changes his way of life, it will lead to spiritual maturity and the continuous activity of the divine powers. The habits of someone who is on the spiritual path, his way of thinking and acting, as well as his character, will completely change. Weariness and idleness decrease. The person becomes selfless and devoted to God. Illnesses are healed or relieved by the inner power. The person's eating habits change and he gradually avoids all animal foods. He also decreases his food intake, and yet he remains fresh, healthy and resilient. On the path of becoming spiritually conscious, a person puts his thoughts into order more and more. He becomes helpful, content and quiet. His whole body comes into harmony. His stride is balanced, his gestures harmonious, and his understanding for the world around him grows. Egoism and selfishness are replaced by the love for God, understanding and love for his fellowman, and the wish to help and to soothe becomes ever greater. Such a person, who is prepared by the inner power, also learns to apply it. He experiences that the Spirit of God is energy, which he may receive by training his will.

As soon as a person entrusts himself to God's guidance, the spiritual streams, the ether powers, become noticeable in the person, they guide and lead the physical body. In many people, the ether powers that are effective in the body are largely latent. This means that their function is very low, because they cannot be addressed by the person. In a God-seeker, these holy powers take on form and shape by expanding the inner body of the soul, and thus, not only show themselves as the guide for the spiritual body, but also as the powers that envelop and protect the physical body. They make the person into a true child of God, namely, a "God-man," who has gradually learned to control himself and can truly serve humankind. Such a person could lead the world to the fount of health of God, provided the worldling would listen to him. In this union of Father and child, it is no longer the human being himself who is active, but rather the Spirit of God, the Father of all children, who is active through His willing instrument. The powers and elements of the universe serve such a person.

Thoughts are the highest powers of creation. When God created the heavenly worlds, there was the "Word," that is, the thought. In reality, it was His sensation of omnipotence. He, the Lord, saw His work already completed.

Every thought should be absolute and bring forth only perfection. In such a divine thought lies the power for completion. The higher a light-thought vibrates, the greater is the resulting positive effect. A divinely pure thought is creative and first finds its echo in the soul before it penetrates into the human being. That is why it is never too soon for a human being to begin to monitor his sensations and thoughts, to weigh and examine them and to strengthen the will, which has become aligned with the divine laws, having been trained so that the divine stream can serve him.

Here, I want to repeat once more, and this is very important: A person must learn to align with God and His will. But if a person trains his self-will, which he wants to use for his own purposes, he is programming his subconscious. These are certain brain cells that are mainly present in the cerebellum. Through this unlawful programming, a person can slip into astral spheres. With this, he does not attract divine forces, but astral beings, that is, souls of deceased people who are still oriented to the Earth. These try to serve him and to fulfill his wishes. Such souls, which are still subject to their base inclinations, have little strength of their own. Since they remain in the spheres of the Earth and want to be active, they try to attract other powers magnetically. They take these either from weak-willed human beings, or from the atmosphere, from the ether chronicle. They then transfer these energies to such people who have programmed their subconscious for selfish purposes. Thus, caution is called for in this regard.

The one who does not invoke these astral forces, but the pure divine forces, must lead a selfless, devoted life, so that these holy Spirit powers can serve him. The astral forces that were attracted from the atmospheric spheres only seem to be useful for the moment; they serve materialistic purposes for only a short time. These negative powers are not beneficial for the soul, but rather make it arrogant and pretentious, which will have to be expiated one day by the soul. Such impure and base forces are not divine powers; they harm the human being who invokes or accepts them.

The person himself does not recognize what is good and beneficial for him. He can recognize this only through the all-knowing ether powers, the all-encompassing law of God, which wants to flow in him and guide him. Therefore, O human being, the alignment is decisive; remember this!

The spiritual forces are also healing forces that every human being can request

The lawful powers of the Spirit are also healing forces, which flow more intensely in a spiritually prepared person and can be transmitted to other people who seek healing, if they are open for them. In this transmission of energies, a contact between the Christ-healer and the one seeking healing takes place, which is triggered by the core of being that is in every soul. This is why true Christ-healers first lay their hands on the back of the head of the one seeking healing, so as to get in touch with the power of God flowing in the person.

If the person seeking healing remains passive and without will during the Christ-healing, without believing in the Inner Physician and Healer, in the law of God that flows in him, there is no closer merging of these spiritual forces. This means that only little energy, or none at all, can flow from the Christ-healer to the one seeking healing. This is why Jesus said: "It will be given to you according to your faith." This means that if a person believes in the Spirit of the Christ of God in his innermost being and surrenders to Him, by aligning with Him, the spiritual contact between the Christ-healer and the one seeking healing takes place.

But Jesus also essentially said: "Go and sin henceforth no more!" This means that if the person falls back into his old habits and vices again, and burdens himself anew, by turning away from the power of God, by again indulging in unlawful ideas without monitoring and controlling his thoughts, he reduces the spiritual power that was transferred to him or that he received through prayer and his own devotion. In this way, old ailments and habits or even greater troubles may appear, because he again reduces this Spirit power, the healing force, with an unlawful way of thinking and acting.

A person does not necessarily need a transmitter of the spiritual power, a Christ-healer. Provided he could move to a higher spiritual level – through the divine training of his will and deep heart-prayer – on which the Spirit power becomes effective without any help from a second or third person, the divine help can directly take place by way of the innermost part of the soul. As I have just revealed, these divine healing forces can be invoked by the person himself, since in every person is the microcosm, the soul, which emerged from the macrocosm, the great totality.

*The correct use of the divine ether powers
that permeate all life forms*

A person on a high spiritual level who knows how to guide these ether powers receives them, not only from within, but also from without, by way of the odic forces, because all Being is based on energy.

Which energy a person requests, and what powers he aligns with is very important. The ether powers are in and around every life form. Every pure life form is ready to serve its neighbor, since serving one's neighbor is lawful. The pure forms of Being actualize the all-encompassing, serving law of God. The mineral, plant and animal kingdoms, too, want to serve people. But since an outwardly oriented person knows little about the divine laws and also does not want to accept them, he violates these life forms, not for his own salvation and well-being, but to the woe and sorrow of his own body and surroundings.

People say, "God, our Lord, lets the herbs grow for the welfare of humankind." However, the lawful streams of God flow through the herbs, which have their true task in the spiritual realm, in the spheres of development. According to the plan of creation, medicinal herbs contain powers that can be invoked, and with which an ill person should align his thoughts, so as to be able to receive their healing forces without having to pick them. Since humankind has lost this connection of unity with all Being, medicinal herbs are gifts of grace from the Spirit, which a person may harvest for healing purposes. Every intake of food is merely an aid, because the activity of the spirit body in the human being is not fully effective.

Unknowing humankind exploits the Earth. It needs raw materials, minerals, and the like. According to the law of God, these are merely powers to be invoked, since their Spirit power is present in the soul of every human being. To be able to positively work and create, a reciprocal action between the specific substance in the soul and in the external world is necessary. The latent ether powers are found in the mineral, as well as in the plant and animal kingdoms. These powers of invocation are not accessible to human beings solely because the children of God disregarded these high powers of creation, and formed and shaped the world according to their own concepts, which were born out of not knowing. Matter is nothing other than a low-vibrating energy field, which has largely repressed the spiritually high energy-potential, enveloping it with weak energies.

Only once the individual turns to God and obeys the principles of the laws of God, subduing everything in love, will the ether powers be able to completely unfold again, by which what has already been revealed would manifest itself. The spiritual body, the ether body, thereby becomes fully effective again, little by little, and will envelop the person as well as the matter. Only then, can it be rightfully said that the Spirit dominates matter.

What can happen in the human being and around him could happen in all material spheres, in the mineral kingdom as well as in the plant and animal kingdoms. The inner, the spiritual structure, would have to turn without in order to dominate the matter. In this way, the entire solar system would gradually come into a higher vibration. In this process, matter would gradually dissolve, and the primordial state, the purely fine-material and spiritual, could emerge. Then, death would no longer exist. There would no longer be any discarding of the shell, of the physical body; instead, the transformation from coarse-material into fine-material substance would take place. However, all this would have to be brought about by human beings, because humankind is the originator of this enormous degree of condensation.

All life forms react to the ether powers. If a person would make use of these high powers, then high powers of light could flow from him that would refine the environment to the degree of his own refinement. The inner ether powers serve a "God-man" who knows how to apply them.

Even *one* lawful thought makes a connection to the All-Life, be it to a plant, or to the mineral or animal kingdoms, by which the corresponding ether powers flow and serve the people. In this way, it would not be necessary to remove large amounts of soil to gain raw materials, or to pick medicinal herbs. Nor would an excessive cultivation of fruits and vegetables be necessary. The spirit substances, the ether powers, are present in infinity, as well as in the human being. They merely need to be addressed properly, and they serve him. Fire, water, earth and air are spiritual as well as earthly elements. If you make use of the spiritual elements, everything will be accomplished through you, provided you are in harmony with God, your Father. From the Spirit's point of view, it is not necessary to displace large amounts of soil, for example, to mine metals, because the substances in the Earth are also in you, in your soul. It would not really be necessary to pick herbs, because the spiritual substance is in your soul. If you can awaken it, it will serve you. A human being would neither have to be cold, nor would he have to earn his bread by the sweat of his brow.

Everything that you need, O human being, is in you! The proper use of these forces would bring forth everything.

All that is condensed must be transformed

Many people who read this revelation and are unknowing will say, "This is utopia. This is not real." Oh, recognize: What a human being does is not lawful, and will not last in the divine reality!

God, your Father, is love.

Whatever a person does that does not come from this absolute love cannot last in the long run. Thinking and acting in a human way alone causes illness, need, distress, and, finally, decay is indicated again and again as the end. Therefore, matter is not eternally existent. This structure will be subject to expansion and dissolution, because the Spirit, the ether power, cannot unfold to bring the person, his Earth and the entire solar system into a high vibration, in order to transform them.

The human being, who is the cause of all unlawfulness, does not change his life. He does not obey the ether power, the Spirit of God, his Father. Thus, these holy powers cannot unfold. Humankind violates this eternally existing, holy ether power on a daily basis, and prevents it from carrying out the assimilation. However, since everything is subject to a lawful process and has to be brought back to its original, eternally pure state, transforming ether powers are now flowing from the Primordial Central Sun via the seven prism suns into all condensed spheres, in order to bring about the refinement and assimilation to the eternally divine. However, since people continue to think and act negatively, and are not willing to first let these divine powers become effective in themselves, this Earth, as well as the soul of the person, has to be released. This means that the Earth's soul will cast off the density, its material garment, just as the person's soul casts off its physical body. This will be accompanied by great disasters. These eruptions of the Earth are the illnesses of the great "Earth-man," of the Earth. The final rebellion of the Earth will take place when the Age of Aquarius comes to an end.

Then, what lasts eternally, the law of love, can become fully effective.

The same is true for the human being. The ill person, too, rebels against his illness and against God, until he collapses after the last rebellion of his body, and thereupon, the soul withdraws. However, in the purification planes, the soul must liberate itself from its unlawful aspects. Only once the soul is purified can the law of love become fully effective in it. Through the pushing power of the Spirit of Christ, who, from His power of Mercy, granted to all of humankind the powers of resurrection, the human being would have the possibilities to prevent this.

However, if the person does not ask for this power, by leading a life according to the will of God, he will be subject to his delusion, and will have to endure unspeakable suffering.

The human being is a child of God, and the person's soul is immortal. Sooner or later, the soul, this eternally creative structure, will have to undergo purification. Every soul will have to someday vivify the ether powers that exist in it, so as to become a true and pure divine child. For a heavily burdened soul, this intense revival and development of these primordial powers can become a path of suffering. Through the sacrifice of Jesus, the Christ, this Earth became a place for souls and human beings to prove themselves and learn. In this school of life, the sincerely seeking soul and the person striving toward God are given the possibility to purify the soul far more quickly than in the spheres of purification, since the ether powers become effective on Earth, provided the human being lives in the law of the Lord and asks for these powers, so that he is able to master matter with the Spirit of God. In order to become aware of this holy power, a righteous way of thinking and acting is necessary.

The one who wants to enter the Kingdom of God has to bring heaven with him

It has already been revealed that the person who wants to undergo a divine spiritual schooling to become a true Christian, a Christian of the inner being, must learn to master his body. The best way to do this is by programming the brain and soul toward God every morning. This programming should be repeated during the day.

Through the powers of recognition of the Spirit, the truly striving God-seeker will also gradually learn what food is good and wholesome for him. The prerequisite for this is that, above all, the person practice self-control and self-discipline and not merely pay attention to his food. In this regard, closely monitoring his sensations and thoughts is important, because a base thought harms a person more than bad eating habits that do not vibrate in the law of God. With negative thoughts, carnal inclinations build up in the soul and in the human being, which induce him to commit base deeds.

The Spirit of life instructs humankind, again and again, to think and act in a positive way, because a negative sensation as well as a likewise negative thought, that is, an impure thought, are the cause of much evil. Food intake is merely secondary here, although it, too, contributes decisively to the fulfillment of the law.

What is decisive, however, are sensations and thoughts. A person can neither read his way into heaven nor eat his way there through vegetarianism! Just as decisive is the development of the ether powers in him, through a way of life according to the laws of God. The soul is measured solely by the fulfillment of these laws.

The one who wants to enter the Kingdom of God must bring heaven with him. Heaven is the purified soul. The soul regenerates only if the person heeds the commandment of life, the commandment of all commandments – love – in all its details. Heaven is the absoluteness, the expression of the highest and purest. It has the highest rate of vibration. Your soul must reach this vibration through a corresponding way of life and bring it along, in order to enter the Father's house, the heavens.

Above all, the heart prayer, in connection with a positive way of thinking and acting, brings about a high vibration of the soul. Harmonious music and light physical exercises also raise the vibration of the soul. At work, you should meet your fellowman selflessly and in a helpful way, and you should do your work well and for the benefit of all. This nobleminded work creates contentment, self-confidence and harmony. With such ways of acting, your body does not become tired as quickly, so that after work, your evening hours go by in harmony. The evening prayer will bear fruit, and attract further Spirit powers, which then serve the resting and sleeping body as well as the soul, which is active also during the night.

The effects of negative thoughts and human conceptions

Often the following question is asked: "What is a negative thought?" Simply the thought that the goods and chattels you have acquired are your property is a negative sensation or a negative thought. The fewest people know that the possessions they believe to have acquired are actually not their own, but are the result of God's grace. The Lord gave the human being the strength to work. The one who thinks differently has already clouded himself with the first negative thoughts and programmed his soul with egoism. His soul clings to the acquired property and is therefore tied to this world. The human being should administer well the gifts of grace that have been granted him, and remain a light-hearted human child who does not bind himself to anything, because he knows that all possessions and goods are merely temporary loans from God.

A person's world of thoughts revolves mainly around his own concerns. The worldly person is mostly preoccupied solely with himself. Thus, he thinks about what he could treat himself to today or tomorrow, in order to benefit his well-being. His striving is to find out what food, what herb or medicine might keep his body flexible, fresh and healthy. This way of thinking already contributes to the reduction of the ether powers that could give him all he needs for his physical and mental well-being. The Spirit, the eternally existing ether power in soul and person, could be his provider and healer.

Through negative, that is, impure, thoughts and human conceptions, the will to do good slackens.

This reduces the divine will power and, as a result, the soul does not find its way to the Godhead. The spirit being, which became a human being over the course of billions of years, no longer recognizes the power and effect of thoughts. The concept of time and space developed through base thoughts that constricted the spirit being and the human being. The farsightedness for the timeless and spaceless was weakened as a result of this limitation. This led to the shadowing of the spirit body and the constriction of the soul and of the human ability to imagine and understand.

Everything is controlled from the human brain, including the eyes. The eyes saw only the vibrations that were condensing more and more, out of which space crystallized and inevitably, units of time developed. The eyes reflect only those things that are programmed in the brain. Just simply humankind's concept of time and space, which was transferred to all material and part-material spheres, resulted in the reduction of the holy powers, through which the mobility of the spirit body, and later of the human being, was impaired, thus losing their connection with the cosmic unity. As a result of this limitation, the human being is no longer able to think in terms of seven divine dimensions, but only in three-dimensional space and time – according to his limitation. Unimaginable as it may sound to human beings, it is the truth, because everything is based on vibration.

If a person believes that God is outside of his self, he will never be aware of God as the God of the inner being, since he lacks the sensitivity for this. Through ignorance and wrong thinking, human beings have built up a world of make-believe in which they believe God to be a strict old man, who sits on His throne above the clouds, living immeasurably far away, separated from His children, and who looks down sternly on them, in order to punish them according to the weight of their faults.

The reaction of the body cells to negative thoughts and medications

Recognize, O human being: God is spirit and the Spirit lives in you. His dynamic power is in every cell of your body. However, if a person feeds his cells with base thoughts and words, and with unlawful food, his cells become purely material cell children.

Just like the soul, the cell structure, too, reacts to every stirring, positive as well as negative. Therefore, the human being should endeavor to develop only highly vibrating thoughts, and to lead a life according to the law of the Lord. Through careless thinking and acting, the person begins to reduce the ether powers in the cells of his body, which causes the cell children, the cells of the body, to become ever weaker and finally, ill. If the cells are not yet accustomed to pharmaceutical medicines, merely the thought, "I will take a medicine," is enough to upset the cell children.

Humankind has not yet explored the power of thoughts. This is why people can analyze neither a positive nor a negative thought, and are thus not able to tell what kind of resonance thoughts trigger in the spiritual as well as in the physical areas. By thinking of a medication, the person no longer gives the Inner Physician, the ether power, the possibility to help and to heal. Since the person does not invoke the divine ether powers, the Inner Physician withdraws, or remains largely latent in the cells of the human body. As soon as the ether power withdraws, the weak cell children's longing for vital energy grows. They open their cell mouths, which means they no longer align with the ether power, but with the medicine that is meant for them, which they take in eagerly. Once they have received a certain dose, they are satisfied as long as the numbing effect of the medicine or its external burst of energy lasts. However, this energy supply does not last long, because everything that comes from without is only of short duration.

What, then, do the ill cell children do, since they are again tired? Through pain and weariness or a craving for food, they ask for more and more. However, the person should remember that noble thoughts are the most natural medicine. The more divine the thoughts are, the more light-filled and healthier is the body of the human being. Negative, that is, brutish sensations and thoughts lead to a reduction of the soul's vibrations, and the body becomes more and more susceptible to illnesses and blows of fate.

As the result of a person's constant wrongdoing, the cells and organs demand more and more medicine and food, as well. The person could keep his body healthy and strong with a much lesser food intake. With a wrong way of life, the person programs his organs and his entire body negatively. With thoughts and actions that do not correspond to the law of God, the blood circulation, the cells, the hormones and glands are brought into a low vibration, that is, they are oriented to the manifestations of this world. In this way a burden, or karma, can build up in the soul over the course of time and break out in later years, or even in a future incarnation.

When the cells, hormones and glands are programmed wrongly, the body demands more and more food and medicine. The base inclinations and cravings increase. The result is that humankind seeks more and more culinary pleasures, thus polluting the cells of their bodies.

Negative effects caused by the exploitation of the Earth and technical achievements

It is essentially written: "Subdue the Earth!" However, this does not mean: "Exploit the Earth." The Lord said: "You shall earn your bread by the sweat of your brow." The all-knowing and wise God spoke these words to a human race that had become crude, that disregarded His law, that craved for more and more, thus polluting the Earth, making the soil largely infertile, and bringing the whole planet into a negative vibration. The "Earth-man," the Earth, which is in the process of dying, cannot nourish people in a pure way anymore and according to the Will of the Lord. The unknowing person goes on acting unkindly and selfishly. By disregarding the divine laws, he robs his Mother Earth of her last strength. The soil, treated with artificial fertilizers, becomes lifeless, because high numbers of the micro-organisms, which should prepare the soil, are killed by these fertilizers. In times to come, the Earth will give less and less food to humankind.

The products overbred by humankind contain only little cosmic power anymore, and are therefore called artificial nourishment by the Spirit of God. This food, cultivated by the people with great effort, does not bear the blessing from the law of God. The artificial fertilization of the soil will become humankind's doom.

The same is true for the machines, airplanes, and engines constructed by human beings. With these achievements, people believe they have created a means of transportation with which they can overcome distance in a short time. In reality, these are all merely aids that they devised, because the soul of the human being became paralyzed, by thinking in terms of time and space, and thus created an unbridgeable gap to the timeless and spaceless realms where there are no distances to be overcome.

This gap to the timeless and spaceless realms will exist until the person and his soul have resorted to the laws of God. Only then, will the soul become aware of its original life in the timeless and spaceless realms. The technical aids disturb the natural events in space and time, binding the soul even more strongly to worldly phenomena and scientific fields.

*Patience, persistence and
devotion in prayers for healing*

O human being, recognize yourself and your doings.

Make the inner power your own, by daily working on yourself.

Examine your life, O human being, your thoughts, words and deeds, and make room for God, the timeless One.

Every negative thought reduces the eternally existing ether power in the soul and in the physical body. Therefore, O human being, program your soul with divine thoughts so that the eternally existing Spirit power can take up its function in your body. Do not rely solely on medicine, but trust the Inner Physician and Healer, who is the all-permeating ether power in you.

A person's daily work should be a constant adoration of God. If you are sick, in prayer, call on the powers of the Inner Physician and Healer, which flow from the fourth consciousness center, located near your heart. Believe in this healing power and go into the stillness, so that the spiritual powers, the Inner Physician and Healer, can become effective. If the Inner Physician and Healer cannot help you immediately, remember that during the course of your lives on Earth, your soul may have become so shadowed that the cell structure of your body is in a low vibration, and consequently, the great Inner Physician and Healer, the eternally existing ether power, cannot help you to the extent necessary. Remember, O human being: Your health depends on the condition, the frequency, of your soul body.

Every engine needs a motive force. First, it must be started up and gain momentum before it can reach its operating level. In the same way, your soul-motor, the soul, must first be brought into higher vibration before it can regenerate the cells of the body. Only once the soul-motor, your soul, increases its activity through the powers of the Spirit, can it supply the cells and organs of your body with increased energy.

But what does the human being accomplish with his impatience? Through intense devotion in prayer to the Infinite, to the eternal Physician and Healer, the human being activates the motor, the soul; but because of his impatience and inability to continue to invoke the divine powers, he prevents increased divine ether powers from flowing in. This negative action is followed by its reaction, and the activity of the soul-motor drops.

Due to this wrong behavior on the part of the person, the Inner Physician and Healer has to largely stop helping, since, instead of praying, the impatient human being reaches much too quickly for external things, like medicine, for example. In many cases, the Inner Physician could quickly become effective, because the soul is not overly shadowed. Through his unknowingness, however, the impatient person hinders the divine activity. He does not give time to God, the Lord, and does not open the door of the soul to the helping inner powers.

With patience, faith and, above all, with prayer, a slight shadowing of the soul can be dissolved very quickly, allowing the ether power to become active.

With childlike faithful devotion and with unshakable trust in the Infinite, increased Spirit powers are released in the soul, which then become effective in the person, in the sick organs. However, the following expression of faith should always be included in each request for help and healing to the Inner Physician and Healer: "Lord, but may Your will be done; Your Spirit will give me relief and healing, provided it is good for my soul."

Be patient, O human being, for God, too, is patient with you, for you shall again become His image.

An example: An older garment has to be cleaned and mended if it is to be decent and look good again. It is similar with your soul and your physical body. The Inner Physician and Healer must free the particle-structure of your soul as well as the cells of your body from negative vibrations and replace them with His noble vibrations, before He can again build up the garment, your earthly shell.

O recognize: The Spirit of God will test the persistence, patience and devotion of the person in all things. Without relying on God, the impatient person reaches for external help, for unlawful food, such as meat, sausage and fish, and for low-vibrating drinks and stimulants like alcohol or nicotine and for medications.

The people of today attach great importance to physical hygiene, health and vitality. Despite modern scientific knowledge, humankind has remained unknowing in terms of the effects of negative thoughts, words and actions. Many people know about telepathy. Nevertheless, the people of this time are unable to notice the effect of the power of thoughts on their own body. Base inclinations and thoughts have a more harmful effect on the soul and on the human being than any medication. Humankind believes that the body can be kept healthy through hygiene, vacation and high-power food alone. For the health-conscious person, every cell of the body is a valuable building block, which he cares for, through a corresponding lifestyle, thus keeping it vigorous – so he believes. And yet, it has not occurred to him that with every negative thought and every unlawful inclination he injures his valuable treasure, his physical body, thus bringing the building blocks, the cells, into disharmony.

Remember, O human being, that thoughts are powers. Ask your Lord and God to bless all life forms, including you. Talk to your cell children in a positive, uplifting manner, because the reciprocal action of "plus" and "minus," and therefore, the life, is in every cell of your body. For this reason, speak to your body's cell children and lead them into a life of health and strength. Each of the cell mouths ought to thirst for the power of God. The human being can influence every cell of his body in a positive or negative way, thus bringing them into a corresponding vibration. Even the craving for foods can be influenced through will power, and by invoking the Lord. Just as the person can establish a spiritual communication with every cell of his body, he can also do this with every one of his organs, because the divine ether permeates all Being and can therefore be invoked.

In everything, orient yourself to the divine and you will receive His life for strengthening and healing. Do not give in to every craving right away, instead, curb yourself and be moderate.

Pray to God, your Father, and entrust every cell of your body to Him, so that His powers can become effective. If humankind would feel and think in a pure and noble manner, the cell structure of the body could recover and build up, thus becoming healthy. The one who has realized that every cell reacts to heart prayers, because the divine life is in every cell, knows about the treasure of his inner being, about the great Spirit, who can direct and guide all things, but can also heal a sick body. A divine and lawful attitude toward life could not only make humankind healthy, but also the Earth.

The knowing person can make use of the upbuilding odic forces of all life forms

God, the Lord, as it is said, had the herbs grow for the benefit of humankind. On the whole, as already revealed, this is correct. However, the Lord did not have them grow for excessive use, because the plant species, too, are to develop into a higher life form.

Every herb belongs to a spiritual collective, and, in the course of eons, contributes to the formation of new soul-units.

Whether it be herbs, vegetables, other foods or medicines, human beings know no moderation. Their cells demand more and more from Mother Earth, and with this, from its rate of vibration.

The human being says that the Earth is over-populated and that humankind needs an ever-increasing share of the Earth's surface for the cultivation of food. The individual person hardly ever thinks about why the Earth is over-populated. A short remark in this context: If the soul were in a higher spiritual vibration upon leaving the physical body, it would not long for this Earth anymore. It would have been released from all earthly desires, drives, vices or eating habits.

Moderation should be practiced in all things, including health-giving herbs. As I have already briefly mentioned: Herbs are enveloped powers of a collective, which develops into higher ether forms in the course of the cycle of eons. Healing with herbal products, herbal teas and the like is merely an aid, because the human being is not able to make use of the inner spiritual powers. Every herb is a cosmic building block, O human being, as it can also be found in your soul. The Creator-God, who is your Father, has created and given cosmic children, whose soul-structure contains the entirety.

The human being does not lead a God-devoted and God-filled life. This is why the inner powers do not serve him. Therefore, he turns to the enveloped ether powers, to herbs, vegetables, fruits, juices and the like. The ether powers will serve the person only once he has recognized the laws of God and applies them to himself and in his daily dealings with his neighbor.

The rate of vibration of each plant is in every human soul. This power can be addressed and activated by every spiritually developed person.

However, if the person settles for only those things offered by the external world, and believes that he has to take medications or large quantities of food to become or remain healthy, he not only reduces his soul's energies with this way of thinking, but at the same time reduces the spiritual power in every herb that he takes. Since the effect of external remedies quickly diminishes, the unsatisfied cell children thirst for more and more. The entire mineral and plant kingdoms are components of the pure spiritual creation, and therefore, have a positive and constructive vibration when they are taken in the awareness that God is the Giver of all that is good. All life forms are spiritual collective powers and are offered from God's garden to humankind for its well-being, and not for exploitation.

All matter is permeated by the spiritual atoms and maintained by their energy. The differently vibrating ether powers, which the spiritual types of atoms emanate, hold the spiritual worlds as well as matter together. They guarantee an upbuilding life, provided a person does not violate these lawful powers.

However, the life forms of the herbs would have a much higher rate of vibration and thus, an even stronger healing effect, if the person partaking of these medicinal herbs would be aware that it is God, the Lord, who has them grow for his well-being.

The infinite power in all things is the all-permeating ether spirit, God, the life. This holy power can become effective unhindered only in those who turn to it and follow the laws of the Lord for the most part.

By turning to the All-power, fewer herbs would be picked. This would result in their spiritual radiation becoming even more compact and life-promoting. As already briefly explained, all of nature receives increased odic forces, especially during the night when human thoughts are resting and humankind's hectic activities subside. These odic forces have an upbuilding and maintaining effect on all life forms. These ether powers are given by the Creator-God, by the Primordial Central Sun, via the prism suns. They flow via the spiritual development spheres into the Earth's soul, which then passes on the odic forces to all good and open vessels. A knowing person will therefore gather the herbs before, during or shortly after sunrise and put them in a shady, quiet place at home. During the drying process much fresh air should blow around them, since especially the air contains spiritual atoms which keep the odic forces of the herbs active for the most part. Later, the drying process can be continued in the house or apartment.

Many radiations influence the energy fields of human beings

The human being consists of several energy fields that are similar to the structure of the Earth and its energy fields.

As all of nature, the human being is suffused with energies that he calls magnetic currents. These are highly potentiated powers that are influenced, above all, by the human way of thinking and acting.

When people move large amounts of earth, they thereby change the radiation tendency of their dwelling planet, the Earth.

This altered radiation influences the magnetic fields and magnetic currents.

Therefore, every displacement of large amounts of earth changes the frequency, and thus, the rate of vibration of these energy currents.

The person oriented solely to without perceives every change of vibration, and reacts accordingly.

I repeat: The magnetic currents suffuse all of matter, and therefore the human being, as well. The worldly person reacts considerably to the constant changes in the magnetic currents. This is why many people are in a different mood each day. The spiritual interaction, the activity of "plus" and "minus," exists in every cell. Consequently, every cell attracts the positive as well as the negative.

A person can therefore magnetize himself with powers of spiritually higher or lower vibration. He constantly strives to attract these different frequencies, and to burden himself with them. These frequencies cast a shadow on his disposition, thus influencing his sensations, thoughts, words and actions.

As I stated at the beginning, ineffably many rays strike the human being: the frequencies of the magnetic currents, the radiations and vibrations from the astral spheres or of souls living directly in the world, all cosmic radiation, that of the planets, of the sun, moon, etc., and the pure, high powers of the home worlds, as well.

All these forces can exist only because they are maintained by the primordial power.

Once a person turns away from the external world and all these radiations, and turns to the primordial eternal power, these radiations are sorted out. The purely cosmic radiation becomes stronger, and supersedes the vibrations that influence negatively. In this way, the person reaches the energy field of the purely spiritual. The energy fields of the person, which thus far were inclined to the Earth and its constantly changing radiations, align with the primordial power.

The result is that the soul as well as the person come into higher vibration, and prefer the life of the

Spirit to the worldly one. The body of such a person becomes lighter and more buoyant, healthy and joyful. Depressions recede, fearlessness increases. This means that the person is expanding his consciousness.

This is why it is mentioned again and again: Only when a person changes and turns to the eternally existing, high energy field, will the base forces of this Earth also be reduced because the person feels, thinks and acts differently. The Earth need not be exploited to the same extent as has been done thus far, because the person is satisfied with what he has received and becomes more and more frugal. He recognizes that his homeland is not this world, but the eternal world of the Spirit, which his soul will enter one day, provided it is cleansed and pure.

Dead food and the heavenly elixir of life

Everything a person needs could be raised from his cosmic-dynamic soul.

To obtain these spiritual powers, absolute devotion to God and His eternal life is necessary. The person would have to desist from his desire to be and to have, and serve his neighbor more. Among the true children of God, there may be neither borders between countries nor people of high rank, but only true brothers and sisters who recognize only one Regent and serve Him: God, the existing ether power, the Spirit that flows throughout all things. With this life in God, the person could address the four spiritual-divine elements that are in all things. The core of being in the elements would answer via the elements and would bring forth everything that the person needs.

However, through its externalized behavior, humankind has marked its environment negatively and has transformed its food down to its present range of vibration. Unlawful food can also have a burdening effect on the soul.

The Spirit calls meat and fish dead food. It is preferred by people who have lost themselves in the low vibration of this world.

Since everything is based on vibration, and thus, everything vibrates and pulsates, the human being and his soul can "infect" themselves with a lower or higher vibration. Not only thoughts and words cause a lasting resonance in the soul and the physical body, but also foods that do not correspond to the laws of God. Unbelievable as it may sound, the human being also eats and drinks his vibration and "infects" himself with it.

The legion of cells aligns with drinks, foods and medications and is thereby infected. A person says: "This drink, this food, or this medicine is good for this or that organ of my body." Simply with these words, he programs his body, causing his cell children to adjust themselves to a certain kind of food, medicine or drink. Since everything is based on vibration and the cells are infected by low vibration, they transform down the power with this or that unlawful intake of energy, thus reducing the Spirit power that flows in them.

The Creator has given human beings a much longer life on Earth.

The ether is the best, the purest and the highest nourishment. The spirit being, the soul in the human being, once partook of this nourishment. The ether is the elixir of life for all pure beings. One day, every soul will again drink consciously from this holy source. Happy the soul and the person who can, little by little, adjust to these sources even today, and who recognize this source, the law of God, as their main nourishment, who align with it and make use of it already during their life on Earth.

The law of cause and effect

With its entrance into this life on Earth, the soul already sets the course it will take on this Earth, its life's clock, thus programming itself to a certain constellation of planets. However, if during the course of his life, the person embarks on the path to the divine, to his higher self, the soul purifies through this way of living, and the cell structure reaches a higher vibration. As a result, the person's breathing process slows down and the earthly lifetime of the body can be extended, because the existing karmic burden can be largely absorbed by the Spirit of God through the devotion to the Infinite. Since the environment vibrates negatively, and therefore, most people cannot adjust themselves consistently to the absolutely pure, the ether powers, time runs out for most Earth-children at the time programmed by the constellation of planets.

God, the Lord of life, helps the human being by way of the core of being in the soul. The Lord offers the person His help via this core of being. Every soul lives eternally. God-Father, gave the soul its form; it is thus ether, which became form and is permeated and maintained by the flowing ether. The spirit being lives and is active through these ether powers. It is therefore completely free and mobile in all of infinity.

With his low-vibrating thoughts and inclinations, the human being has transformed down the pure ether energy, thus confining himself. As a result of these low vibrations, illnesses developed, which formed into soul-burdens, into karma. This is what the soul and person now live with.

If the soul-burden does not flow out during a life on Earth, after its physical death, the soul takes this burden along into the soul realms and from there – if there is a further incarnation – again into another life on Earth. Unknowing and thoughtless, still blinded by its former ideas, the soul often inflicts more burdens on itself, which sooner or later break open like an abscess, and pour into the cell structure via the person. Thus, illnesses or disturbances of the general condition often appear whose cause cannot be found. The person then asks himself, "Where do these illnesses come from and why am I, of all people, plagued by this?" If humankind had been informed about the law of cause and effect, the law of karma, many people would bear their fate more easily, and above all, would avoid creating further causes.

Since the person is not instructed about the lawful consequences of his own negative actions, he thinks that his illness was brought about by coincidence. Because of this ignorance, the soul often cannot find its way out of the wheel of reincarnation for a long time.

Many instructions by the Spirit were common knowledge in this world. However, only the fewest people make use of these truths through their own efforts.

*Killing and consuming animals
leads to soul burden*

Everything is based on vibration. Simply with eating habits that are not in accordance with the law, causes can be created that reduce the vibration of the cells, making them unable to absorb the necessary substances. As revealed, these low-vibrating foods are mainly meat and fish.

In the Holy Scripture it is written: "You shall not kill." This commandment refers not only to human beings but also to the animal kingdom.

Many people will say, "A selection has to be made." To this, let the following be said: If humankind had not reduced the high, eternal law by interfering in the law of God and making its own laws and privileges, there would be a very natural, lawful balance. However, since the ecological balance is disturbed, the animals mate at shorter intervals. Breeding could also be controlled by the law of the Lord, but since the ether powers have withdrawn more and more, because humankind let its arbitrariness prevail, everything has gotten out of divine order. Moreover, many animals are bred to be slaughtered. Such actions cause negative resonances in the atmosphere, in the Earth and in human beings that cannot even be described in detail. These low-vibrating forces, which can never again unite with the primordial power, not only vibrate in space, but – and this is very decisive – also in the human body.

As I have already frequently revealed: All that is base and unlawful originates from the human being. People change the rate of vibration of their own bodies, of the Earth-body, of the atmosphere and, in the end, of the entire solar system. These unlawfully limiting vibrations, which originate from human beings and are not accepted by the primordial power, are transferred to the people's surroundings. They once produced the three dimensions, space, in which the positive as well as the negative falls back on the one who caused it.

Anyone who eats excessive amounts of dead, unlawful food on a daily basis becomes complicit of killing, and burdens not only his physical body, but also his soul. Such a habit can build up a soul debt. Furthermore, the body becomes lazy and fat over the years, since the cells, glands and hormones slow down their activity.

Many of our brothers and sisters will say: "But if I do not know about these things, I cannot burden myself."

However, it is written: "You shall not kill!" If the human being consumes excessive amounts of animal food, he becomes an accessory to the killing. Thus, he is acting against the commandment. However, it will not only burden the unknowing person who consumes this unlawful food, but most of all, those people will have to account for their actions who call themselves servants of the Lord, but teach the all-encompassing truths of God only within the limit of human dogma. This is why the Lord said, among other things: "The blind lead the blind, and both fall into the pit."

At all times, the Spirit of God tried to explain to humankind the law of cause and effect. However, people did not listen to enlightened men and women, but to their blind leaders who exercised, and still exercise, great power over their sheep. This power was, and still is, granted only by the unknowing people who believe them blindly without sufficient examination.

The one who wants to enter the heavenly realms must bring the inner heaven with him. Heaven or hell is within every person. The one who purifies his soul lets heaven arise in it. He makes the high ether powers, the law of God, flow, by feeling, thinking, speaking and also acting according to the instructions of the Lord. However, the one who binds himself to this Earth alone, and gives his human habits free rein, will create his own hell. He will have to live in the torments caused by himself, already in this life, in the spheres of purification or in a future incarnation.

All food that is not based on the law of God is not only disadvantageous for the body, but also for the soul. Over time, all animal foods, but also alcohol, nicotine, medicines, drugs and the like, lead not only to a soul debt and to a pollution of the cell structure, but also – and this is very essential – to a continual increase of ignoble sensations, thoughts, words and deeds, which are reflected in the world karma. Because of these constant infringements, the soul and body do not vibrate in the high frequency of the divine ether.

The so-called world karma consists of the merged auras of cities and nations. This karma of the world finds its expression in the atmospheric chronicle and influences human concepts about the world. Revelations on this subject have already been frequently given. Every event, positive as well as negative, is registered in this atmospheric chronicle and shows its effects sooner or later.

Incorrect preparation and usage of farmland

The excessive cultivation of vegetables and various kinds of lettuce is not lawful. Aside from vegetables, this also includes primarily wheat, rye, barley, oats, etc. This excessive cultivation weakens the Earth, because its lawful rhythm is disturbed.

The Earth is prepared by the interaction of the sun, moon and planets. The planetary connections give the Mother Earth high energies, through which the land for food, the soil, is stimulated for further fertilization. An excessive consumption of these high energies makes the earth infertile, and the great "Earth-man" dies because his children deplete him. Neither chemicals nor irrigation is useful here. Only a lawful behavior will help. The best care and cultivation of the earth is the introduction of periods in which the land lies fallow, for one or several years, between the individual cultivation periods of the soil. The microorganism, which could develop during these rest periods of the soil, would prepare the arable land. Some of these small or even tiniest "nature cleaners" create channels of irrigation which guide the confluence of the rainwater. Others prepare and aerate the soil, so that the roots can go deep into the earth and thus better nourish and invigorate what has been sown. The particles of the sun and the moon, which carry high energies of fertilization, also remain for a very long time in such fallow soil. So people not only kill the animals to satisfy their palates, but also those, which through a lawful radiation, could become active in and on the soil, in order to prepare the soil, its aeration and the course of the water.

And so, the great "Earth-man," the Earth, is exploited by its children until it gradually grows weak, vegetates and finally dies. As revealed: Fertilizers and irrigation are useless in this case. Only a complete turnabout will help, away from the path into ruin and to the eternal law of God, which bears within all that a person and his soul need for a true, healthy life. An example:

If a woman on the Earth were to give birth to a child year after year, her body would become slack, tired and sick, because it could not so quickly produce the substances it needs to become strong again.

It is the same with Mother Earth. Year after year she is depleted more and more. Where should she find the strength to recover? The answer is: Only in the cyclic course of the planets and their interaction. The rays of the planets and the elements that fertilize the Earth in collaboration with "nature's cleaners" cannot ever become effective so quickly, because they, too, are subject to the laws of the eternally existing ether. The law of God does not conform to the human way of thinking and acting. The eternally existing law is perfect and gives according to immutable conditions. Therefore, humankind would have to adjust if it does not want to slip even more deeply into ruin.

Animal foods develop sensuality, a hard heart and brutality in human beings

Everything vibrates and pulsates. Every thought can create – as revealed – a positive or a negative cause. The same is also true of food. Dead food, that is, meat and fish, have a very low vibration. Over the course of a lifetime, this vibration settles in the cell structure of the body and gradually influences it negatively.

The attentive observer recognizes and experiences this to some extent in the animals of the forest, of the fields and the air, as well as with his domestic animals. If an animal feeds on too much meat, it becomes fierce and wild, and in many cases, can no longer live freely in the house or in the immediate surroundings of people. It is similar with human beings. The person becomes hard-hearted, brutal and cruel, not only toward the animal and plant kingdoms, but also toward his neighbor. By constantly thinking and acting negatively, humankind became the predators of the animal and plant kingdoms. And among their own kind, they become violent and, in many cases, are worse and more unrestrained than a wild animal hunting for prey.

Over the course of a lifetime, the non-divine actions burden the soul and also influence the person's disposition. Simply with an uncontrolled way of eating, which reduces the high power of vibration of the Spirit, a person can become aggressive and unrestrained, even mentally disturbed. The vibrations of negative foods strike certain stimulation zones in the body that may trigger sensuality, anger, hatred, envy, a penchant for drugs, murder, and all sorts of cravings.

Unlawful thoughts, as well as negative foods create causes that can have unforeseen effects for the person and his soul. Every negative stirring and action settles in the soul and envelops and influences it negatively. An unlawful way of thinking and acting and a low-vibrating negative diet are, among other things, the greatest opponents of human beings.

Thus, the enemy of the human being is not to be sought outside of him, but it is the person himself. Every individual is his own enemy, since the negativity originates in him and not, as many people think, in the Earth, in animals, or even in God, who allegedly punishes the human being. God, the Lord, merely allows the effects of a person's wrong conduct, so that over the course of time, the human being, or the soul in the spheres of purification, recognize his own faults and is thus stimulated to repent and atone. Without recognition of one's own guilt, there can be neither repentance nor atonement. Therefore, the person and soul must recognize their own weaknesses so that these can be eradicated.

However, a person will not find his way to God, our Father, with a vegetarian diet, alone. Through his negative ways of thinking and acting, a person often debilitates what he has built up in his body by eating appropriate food. Thus, he remains his whole life long on the same spiritual level, despite good and lawful eating habits.

If a person thinks and acts positively, and yet maintains his body with a small quantity of meat and fish, he can often mature spiritually more quickly than a fanatical vegetarian who thinks only of his body and neglects the instructions for the development of his soul.

However, if a person endeavors to walk the spiritual path consistently, the inner power of God will slowly release him from his still existing craving for foods, and especially for animal food, and lead him to what is natural. Later, once the aspirant is on the ascetic path, the God-seeker can – in addition to his earthly food – ask for the ether powers of the soul, which contain all the spiritual substances of life from the nature kingdom.

*Prayer releases energies –
Fanaticism causes harm*

The law of God, the flowing ether Spirit, is the bearer of all the powers of the universe. With these ether powers, all the atoms in the entire creation, and in every form of ether are nourished. Thus, the law of the Lord is the healer and helper, in fact, even the provider of the human being, if he applies the law accordingly.

At this point, the heart prayer has to be mentioned.

Prayer can be a dialogue with God, our Lord. With a deep heart prayer, also called a prayer of faith, a person releases unimaginable powers in his soul. Provided he makes this prayer his life's prayer, he thus purifies his soul and the body. The divine ether powers, more intensely developed in this way, will then serve the person more and more.

The human being is in his life's prayer when he fulfills the will of the Lord day and night, by putting himself under his own control, by curbing himself in all things and by applying moderation to himself, and by not giving his thoughts, as well as his words and actions free rein. Daily self-monitoring and self-analysis also includes the control of the food intake. Curb your eating habits and do not indulge in gluttony; instead, consider what is important for your body and also serves the well-being of your soul.

Once more it should be emphasized: If a person aspires to the ether powers as his high goal, he should not become fanatical. All fanaticism is harmful, especially when a person is following the spiritual path. Ask the Spirit of God for guidance, O human being, so that the inner Spirit purifies its temple little by little, and soul and person become free. However, the person must support this process of purification with lawful thoughts and actions.

Self-chastisement does not dissolve cravings – Repression and its incalculable consequences for the soul

A person should not chastise himself. This would be completely wrong. As long as cravings of the palate can still be noticed, for example, they should not be repressed completely.

Often, a person suffers from a severe illness or the body is so weakened that it needs medications.

If the person takes them, he should carefully consider how high a dose is absolutely necessary. The patient should bless them before they are taken and should try to reduce the dose little by little. The compensation would be in the devotion to God and the deep prayer of faith.

When a person chastises himself, this does not mean that the cravings are obliterated. Sooner or later, that is, perhaps after many years, or when the soul is discarnate, these repressed tendencies break out again. It could be that now, the soul has to suffer greater pain than it would have if the cravings had been gradually and lawfully reduced during its life on Earth. If such repressed habits are released one day, it is possible, for instance, that a soul in the astral spheres sets off to cling to people who indulge in the same proclivities in their life, for instance, the consumption of lots of meat and fish, taking medicines, drugs, nicotine, alcohol, and the like, etc. A soul with negative inclinations can even stimulate a very outwardly oriented person to more unlawful actions, merely to delight in these and to assuage its cravings as a soul.

Often, several souls that have taken their lusts of the palate and cravings with them to the soul realms in the beyond are attached to the vibrations emanated by a human being who clings very much to animal foods, or is addicted to nicotine, alcohol, or other vices. A person who leads an unlawful, profligate life is surrounded by souls who live on his level of vibration, and who thirst for all those things to which he is enslaved.

The continuing life of a soul, however, can also take the following course: A profligate and hedonistic life, which could not be overcome on this side of life and was taken along into the beyond, often urges the soul into a new incarnation, because the propensity for an unlawful life is very intense. Because of these negative inclinations, which adhere to the soul, such a soul cannot escape from the wheel of reincarnation, from the pull of matter.

On the other hand, if a person aligns with the divine and asks the Spirit of God for guidance and healing, he increases the activity of the core of being, of the soul.

Such a person aspiring to God, aspiring to the full effectiveness of the divine ether powers in himself, should pay attention to the following: thoughts, words, actions and eating habits. The inner Spirit in the human being will then purify its temple little by little, making the soul and person pure. The person can contribute to this to the degree that he asks the ether powers for support, that he monitors his thoughts and reduces his intake of low-vibrating foods.

What vibrations adhere to animal products and to organic foods?

O human being, to make it easier for you to let go of unlawful foods and to curb the lust of your palate, look at the suffering animal world. It has to suffer so much, also because of *your* negative inclinations. Look at the fearful animals that are brought to the slaughterhouse! The vibrations of fear permeate their entire body and remain in the entire organism. Look at the living beings, crowded together into the most narrow spaces, fattened on your account and thus violated! They do not send out harmonious, positive vibrations. These frequencies also adhere to their flesh, and cannot be reduced by frying, cooking or seasoning! Think also of the animal captors and trappers who likewise often kill animals cruelly so that you, O human being, can adorn yourself with a beautiful fur! Bring to mind the mortal terror of the young animals that are brutally torn from their mothers and killed before their eyes, because vanity is more important to human beings than the life of the animals. All these vibrations adhere to the food and to the furs.

O human being, adorn yourself with the ornament of virtue, with the glorious, compassionate love for your fellowman, and for your second neighbors, the animal and plant kingdoms. Then, you are pleasing to God, your Lord.

Many people strive for food that is free of artificial fertilizers. Concerning this, the Spirit of God says through His servant, Emanuel: As already revealed, everything is based on vibration. Even organic foods are no longer untainted. The poisonous substances in as well as on the Earth and in the atmosphere also affect the foods that were grown without artificial fertilizers. It is an error to think that with organic foods alone, the body can be kept healthy. This is a fallacy of unknowing humankind. With foods that are free of artificial fertilizers, a person possibly builds up a higher vibration in his body, but he reduces it again with base thoughts, words and actions. The whole Earth, and also the atmosphere, is polluted with the unlawful actions of people.

Many people will not understand me. Therefore, I again repeat: If a person cultivates food without artificial fertilizers and tends to it accordingly, the food does indeed have a higher value measured by its vibration. But this is often transformed down by the producer's negative ways of thinking and acting, and thus, remains on the same level as the forms of life treated with artificial fertilizers. First, the producer should undertake self-recognition, if he provides people with food who place great value on organic foods:

"What is my radiation like and what is my motivation for growing vegetables and fruit? Is my main concern to earn a lot of money, or is it the health of my fellowman?"

All life is based on vibration.

To give rise to a healthy life and pure growth, a conscious way of life is necessary, also for the people who grow and sell fruits and vegetables. Every life form needs the two poles, positive and negative. Through cosmic influences, an interaction between these two powers takes place, through which life develops.

An electrical source can flow and produce light and power only when such an interaction exists. It is the same with all life forms. This interaction exists in every cell of the body, in every atom, as well as in fruits and vegetables.

If vegetables, fruits, herbs and the like are to grow and flourish correctly, that is, lawfully, the correct positive and negative charge must be present.

To bring the high ether powers into unfoldment in the foodstuff already during cultivation, the person should pay attention to the vibration of his thoughts and words.

Every life form, including plants, is permeated by high energies, which are reduced very easily by improper handling. Since everything is based on vibration, the unlawful frequency emitted by a person can very quickly diminish the ether power in the plant. If, for instance, organically grown vegetables or herbs are cut off or plucked carelessly and for self purpose only – just as those grown with artificial fertilizers – this action alone reduces the flowing ether power in the plants.

Every form of Being lives and feels in its own way, that is, according to its state of consciousness. Ask yourself, O human being, if someone would approach you brutally with a knife or a rifle in his hand, how would you react, and what vibrations would come up in you? Your reaction would be fear!

Similar vibrations radiate from the entire plant and animal kingdoms when they are treated brutally, selfishly and hardheartedly. These fearful, low vibrations, which trigger a shock reaction, settle not only in your soul, O human being, but also in the souls of the other plants and animals, in fact, in all life forms.

The kingdoms of the plants, as well as animals, have very fine and high rates of vibration, since these life forms cannot burden themselves. In accordance with their consciousness, they also know no fear. Only when a brutal vibration intrudes, do the plants and animals react with anxiety or fear. Every vibration, the positive as well as the negative, produces a corresponding resonance in the bodies of human beings and animals as well as in plants.

All of nature, the herbs and all the different kinds of fruits and vegetables, react to positive and negative vibrations. Negative vibrations reduce the high ether powers that stream through nature. This is why the nutritive value of plants is frequently no longer high, because the vibrational effect, the increased ether power, is missing. The Spirit cannot possibly describe the detailed interrelations of this interaction more specifically, because humankind has neither coined the words nor the concepts that would make it possible to present the details clearly and distinctly.

O human being, remember that the reactions of grief and fear also vibrate in the body cells of the animal that is taken to the slaughterhouse. People absorb these negative vibrations with the meat they eat.

A predator that feeds mainly on meat reacts brutally and aggressively. The behavior of a person who eats meat is similar. The result is: aggression, fear, hatred, murder, faulty reactions, wars and destruction all over the Earth and in the atmosphere. Then, these reactions are even intensified by unknowing souls from the worlds of the beyond, which tend very much toward matter, because when they were human beings, they lived immoderately and dissolutely.

The law of the Spirit is: Like attracts like. Thus, more emotions and sensuality are invariably stimulated by the excessive consumption of meat.

Humankind is annihilating itself

The radiation from the arsenal of atomic weapons and from nuclear power plants, and the enormous level of noise on this Earth, in the air, and in the water, tear up the magnetic fields of the Earth and displace them. Consequently, the cosmic irradiation from the planets falls on other parts of the Earth's magnetic field. This process contributes to a change in humankind, in the animal and plant kingdoms, as well as in the entire dwelling planet, Earth, because the magnetic currents penetrate all life forms.

Scientists who are oriented solely to matter and church authorities who have greatly slipped into worldliness are ultimately to blame for this gradual destruction of humankind as well as of the entire

Earth. The Christian churches as well as the scientists have led and lead humankind onto a path of spiritual ignorance. Because of their claim to authority, the masses that have become blind to the spiritual laws now look more and more to what they do and say. Thus, the pit of ignorance, foolishness and human arrogance grows ever wider. Soon, many of these blind ones, that is, all those who believe in this worldly wisdom and are bound and still bind themselves to matter alone, will fall into this pit.

If all of a person's aspiration and striving is based solely on the external life, he is often no longer capable of applying the laws of the Lord. Through his continuous wrongdoing and acting against the laws of the Lord, the person reduces the ether powers that flow in his body. Thus, he needs higher quantities of food, in order to be able to absorb the necessary energies, minerals, carbohydrates, and so forth.

The human being has lost the right measure in all the things of life. As a result, the Earth, the dwelling planet of humankind, is exploited and defiled. The perpetrator, humankind, is presented with the invoice for all this, and God, the Lord – so humankind thinks –

should pay it. Oh, no! The bill is presented to humankind and humankind must pay it, itself.

The human being can regain his health only if he abides by the laws of the Lord, also in regard to the plant and animal kingdoms

The helper, the Inner Physician and Healer, is the law of God, the ether power in all existing forms of being, including the human being. Only with devotion to God, can a person regain his health through the eternally existing life force.

Recognize yourself, O human being, for you are a child of God! Provided that a person is aware of his filiation to God and shapes his life according to the laws of God, by heeding the law of the Lord in himself and toward his neighbor, he will also regain his health according to the will of the Lord.

Ask God for His guidance in prayer!

The refinement of a person can be successful only if he does not give in to every inclination for the lusts of the palate and libidinousness. Remember, O human being, that sensations, thoughts, and words are unimaginable powers that can create causes or nullify them. It depends on the right application. There is a saying: "Do not do to others what you do not want them to do to you!"

Would you, O human being, like your neighbor to torment, torture and kill you? How would you react if you were brutally robbed of your land, and the robber threw you on a wagon like a worthless piece of wood and took you away? Yet, this is just what people do. They fatten animals for slaughtering, cramming them together in the closest quarters and rob them of their freedom. They are tormented in the cruelest way, without any scruples, in order to achieve a favorable price. Likewise, vegetables, fruits and grains etc., are cultivated in excessive quantities and forced to heightened growth through the use of artificial fertilizers. At harvest time, the ripe fruits and the grains are brutally taken from the soil, and cabbages, lettuces, and other vegetables are thrown on the truck and supplied for a thoughtless mass-consumption.

O human being, recognize yourself! Have you not become the greatest predator on this Earth?

What does the Inner Physician and Healer, the law of the Lord, the true giver of life in you, say about this? As long as a person acts unkindly and only egotistically, neither his soul nor his body can regain health. Not only the person and soul suffer under this human ignorance and cruelty, but also the entire dwelling planet, the Earth, which will become a wasteland over the course of the times to come.

Thoughtlessly treated natural products reduce their energy-giving qualities

All Being is based on vibration. Humankind is not familiar with the subtle points of this divine law. The vibrations that people can measure are based only on their coarse world of sensations. Just as coarse and negative as the nature of human beings has become, so, too, is their reaction to the environment, to the Earth and, not lastly, to the entire solar system.

Many vegetarians who are concerned solely with their body think that they render their body a great service by choosing natural products, vegetables and unsprayed fruits as their main source of food. But they rely more on the natural products than on the Spirit, the ether law in human beings. The Inner Physician and Healer, the law within the person, says the following to this: Naturally fertilized vegetables and unsprayed fruits may have a somewhat higher vibration than sprayed fruits and artificially fertilized vegetables. However, as the result of the overall pollution of the Earth and of the atmosphere, these vegetables and fruits are also suffering, because the subterranean springs, the rain, the drinking water – everything – has been polluted by the human beings, and this pollution will finally fall back on them and on the natural products.

All Being lives because the ether Spirit, God, permeates everything. The one who treats the divine life forms unkindly creates negative resonances in them, thus diminishing their rate of vibration. Even if it is vegetables free of artificial fertilizers and unsprayed fruits, any life form that is treated unkindly by an unenlightened person reduces its energy-giving qualities. When plant products are handled just as brutally as animals, they likewise suffer a trauma, just like the animals. As a result, the ether power can no longer become fully effective because everything in the entirety of creation reacts even to sensations. Every plant, even the most inconspicuous, bears God's seed of life. If these bearers of life are disturbed, that is, if they are touched with negative vibrations, even a simple vegetable plant reacts. This means that it takes up a defensive position by sending out negative vibrations, which changes the nutritional value, as already revealed. The same is true for herbs and all kinds of fruit.

Even though these explanations may sound unbelievable to the human being, may they be nevertheless expressed. Until today, people still do not recognize what negative resonances are, which are ultimately caused by human ignorance, since people cannot recognize the power of their own thoughts, words and actions.

Of certain animals, for example, people know that they release unpleasant substances when they are touched. This happens, more or less, with every plant, vegetable and fruit as well as with *every* animal.

Therefore, even if natural products have a higher rate of vibration and their nutritional value is correspondingly high, this is diminished by people's brutal handling of plants. Without first considering whether fruits, vegetables, plants or animals are momentarily being charged lawfully with energy or not, they are carelessly torn from the soil, from the tree or the shrub. The animal is killed, and its flesh is prepared as food for people.

Ask yourself, O mother, how your baby would react if you were to brutally tear the bottle of milk from his mouth and hands?

How does a running engine react when you suddenly block it?

In every life form there are the two life poles, positive and negative. When these carriers of life are disturbed by the thoughts or actions of people, unlawful vibrations develop in them. Through this, the somewhat higher vibrating natural product grown without artificial fertilizers is also harmed, that is, the somewhat higher vibrating life form is thereby transformed down. All these vibrations, which were generated by people, will sooner or later fall back on them, on their soul and on the Earth.

Especially high ether powers at sunrise are active for human beings and the harvest

During nighttime, between 10:00 PM and 3:00 AM, the Spirit power and also the planets of the solar system generously supply the whole Earth, with all its phenomena and life forms – including the human being – with life energies.

The human being is a product of his Earth. The composition of the human body is water and Earth. These two components likewise receive high life forces from the eternal spheres of energy. They are supplied to the body via the consciousness centers and the nerve pathways. This is why sleeping before midnight is best, because during this time, the high cosmic energies are granted to all of matter abundantly.

Therefore, at sunrise, human beings, animals, vegetables, fruits and plants are charged with highly potentiated ether powers. It is advisable to harvest plants, fruits and vegetables, as well as grains, particularly at this time. The one who harvests the vital products in the early morning and according to the law of life receives not only a more highly vibrating nourishment, but he receives high odic forces in addition, which are especially active in nature during the early morning hours. In this way, increased Spirit powers build up in the human being and in the soul.

The one who knows about these processes and thankfully accepts these holy powers by respecting life, even if it is an inconspicuous animal or a plant, can be certain that he absorbs more energies during the morning hours than if he takes it easy all day long, works little and uses natural products as his nourishment.

The high odic power contains everything that a person needs to live. The odic forces, also called ether powers, strengthen nerves and muscles, build up the cells and bring the hormones into consonance, give life forces to the organs, regulate digestion, affect the function of the intestines, and thus, harmonize the entire body, which it needs to remain healthy and vigorous. The prerequisite is, however, that the ether powers flow in the person's soul and body in accordance with the divine law. Thus, in reality, it is the ether power that is the nourishment for the soul and, figuratively speaking, also for the physical body. And so, the human being can breathe in his fill already early in the morning.

How can the vibration of "auxiliary food" be built up?

Since the human being no longer knows how to apply these ether powers, God, our Lord, gave him auxiliary food for the well-being of his earthly body. They are the condensed life forms, which he calls grains, fruits, vegetables, etc., whose rate of vibration corresponds to the condensed earthly structure of the human being. This means, in turn, that the food of the human being is attuned to the vibration of his body. As already mentioned, God, the Lord, permitted the formation of matter through the thoughts of His children. And through their own thoughts and deeds, they are to be led back again to the origin, the ether form. And so, a person eats and drinks the condensed vibration that he himself created through his thoughts, and that was and is permitted by God, our Lord.

The one who uses the ether power by way of a deep, sound sleep at night and with devotion to the eternal laws in the morning hours will be in good shape throughout the whole day. The one who blesses the fruits of the field and thankfully takes in the All-power in the spirit of God can, if he is in spiritual evolution, build up again the odic vibration of the food that was transformed down by unknowing people.

The heart prayer and its actualization is the highest dispenser of energy

The highest dispenser of energy is the recognition that God is the ether power in all forms of Being.

The best nourishment and the best dispenser of energy is the heart prayer.

Through the heart prayer, the recognition unfolds that in all Being there is life, the high ether powers, and that everything is based on these powers. When a person acknowledges these powers and makes use of these eternally existing lawful life forces, by leading a life according to the laws of God, the holy ether powers will serve him. However, someone who prepares the products of the field without prayer and gratitude, and now devours them as savory food will not spiritually build up his body cells or his soul.

The vegetarian whose only concern is naturally fertilized foods and who does not turn to the holy ether powers or think and act according to the laws of life, will not build up his soul.

The meaning of the instruction "Subdue the Earth" and of the spiritual law "Like attracts like"

It must be pointed out, however, that the one who consumes animal foods reduces the cell vibration of his body to a far greater degree than the vegetarian does. In addition, his soul is burdened, because the highly evolved animals that are slaughtered have a part-soul, which reacts, feels, perceives and flows out in a much more sensitive way than the collective spheres of nature.

The law is valid: "You shall not kill." This commandment from the law of the Lord refers not only to the human being, but applies to all life forms, including the plant and animal kingdoms.

The Lord said: "Subdue the Earth!" With this, He, the great All-One, meant that the human being should act in such a way that the life forms serve him and do not become his curse. If the human being does things that are not lawful, for instance, if he consumes negatively vibrating food, he sets free vibrations that pollute the cells of his body and burden the particle structure of his soul.

I repeat, because this is very essential for insight: Like attracts like. This means that low-vibrating things do not attract high energies and vice versa. If the human being defiles his Earth through negative actions, exploiting it and letting it starve, he does not produce high vibrations. Consequently, the ether powers cannot serve him. In this way, he separates himself from the guidance of the Spirit of God and does not act constructively, but destructively.

Ether power as nourishment instead of the satisfaction of the lust of the palate

Humankind does not align with the all-permeating divine power, but only with the Earth and its events. This is why the soul and the human organism are disturbed. Because of the ignorance of humankind, life is brutally torn from Mother Earth at any time of the day and is prepared at human discretion. With this course of action, humankind will gradually kill the big dwelling planet and finally, himself.

Not only illnesses develop as the result of these actions of ignorance, but also karmic damages, soul burdens. As a result, the law of God can affect and build up the person less and less, because he moves away from God, His Father, more and more. In order to attain the cell vibration necessary to live, the physical body calls for increasingly dense food. The cosmically weak, starving soul demands – by way of the sensations of the palate – the satisfaction of the senses. The loss of spiritual energy increases the lusts of the palate and the person lets this happen without giving it a thought. He increasingly grabs for more and more culinary delights, alcohol, nicotine, drugs, and the like. The body's cells, weak and injured through these base human inclinations, then also call for more medications that are thoughtlessly given to them. Whatever the body's cells call for, the person living in affluence will give them. The ether powers recede more and more in the particle structure of the soul and in the cells of the body.

Since the human being is solely oriented to without and binds himself to the products of this Earth, the cells become more and more dissatisfied. To live, they need upbuilding energies. Because of this, they have an ever-increasing appetite and constantly call for different stimulants. The servile person, who all that willingly satisfies the lust of his palate, gives in to his human inclinations, because he does not know the ether powers as the God-given main nourishment, but considers the Earth to be his sole pasture. All of humankind acts in this way.

Illnesses, physical and spiritual death as the result of wrong thinking and acting

Since the cell children come into low vibration through a wrong way of thinking and acting of the thoughtless human being, they are susceptible to many illnesses that are nothing other than negative vibrations. In the end, they fall ill. As a result of the unlawful conduct of the person, the divine ether power, the Inner Physician and Healer, withdraws more and more, since He is not requested by the person.

In addition to the weak cell structure of the human being, the physical overexertion of a person also takes place. The hectic rhythm nowadays in professional and daily life demands more and more of the human being. The now outwardly oriented person seeks pleasure and luxury as compensation. The cells perceive this human act of will and demand more and more of their person.

Thus, the human being works, driven ever more strongly by his own desires, by his wanting to be and to have. One person drives the other, but in reality, it is, in turn, the starving body cells and the low-vibrating soul which demand more and more. One person strives for wealth, the other for food and stimulants, others strive for sensual enjoyment. Because of this, the cells are in a constant uproar and demand whatever they were oriented to. The driving power is the "satan of the senses" in human beings, and the flagging cosmic soul, which likewise strives only for sensuality and worldly well-being. As a result of the effeminacy of humankind, the ether powers, the law of God, withdraw more and more, because humankind constantly violates this high, serving commandment of love.

With these only outwardly oriented activities, the person moves into his own self-created circle of lingering illness and material and spiritual death.

It is of little use for a person to call: "O Lord, my God, why have You forsaken me?" It would be better if the person would call: "O Lord, my God, why have I forsaken You?"

Jesus of Nazareth said on the cross "My God, My God, why have You forsaken Me?" This statement has a manifold, symbolic meaning. One is that through Jesus, the Son of God, Himself, all of humankind was speaking. He, the Lord, expressed what had already become evident in the hearts of humankind even then, and which is breaking open at this time more intensely. These words expressed the state of humankind living at that time and in the future, for Jesus was a symbol for all people.

PART 2

The Spiritual Vegetarian – Self-Healing of Various Illnesses

Structure and function of the ether body – The soul and the physical body

God is Spirit. The eternally existing ether body of the pure beings, too, the incorruptible body, consists of spirit. The soul, this imperishable body, is composed of five different kinds of spiritual atoms. These five kinds of spiritual atoms form the life in the spiritual particles of the soul, which consist of compressed light ether and are permeated by the flowing ether. The light ether, which continuously stimulates the formation of particles, is a modified power from the pulsating spiritual primordial atom "love." The collective term for the entire creative Being is "ether."

The compressed ether consists of seven times seven spiritual life-paths, also called ether channels. It is a spiritually highly vibrating ether substance that is permeated by the flowing ether, the Infinite.

The soul is attuned to the structure of infinity. It is a microcosm in the macrocosm. This spiritual structure is called spirit being, provided it is free of all worldly inclinations. It bears within itself the entire cosmic process.

The seven times seven ether channels of the soul are arranged like the ether channels of infinity. The ether channels are the supply veins of the spiritual body. Through these spiritual veins flows the streaming ether, which originates in the spiritual primordial atom in the core of being of the Primordial Central Sun. The ether nourishes the particle structure and the five kinds of spiritual atoms within it, the elements. Thus, the soul is an energy body that lives from the ether powers that flow to the spirit being from the Primordial Central Sun by way of the seven times seven ether channels. These forces are conveyed to the elements in the soul particles in the rhythm of the universe. This is what keeps the spirit being, the soul, alive, which is therefore in constant contact with the entire creation.

Through the Fall of the pure spirit beings, seven unlawful garments developed around the changing ether body, the soul, which hindered the soul from taking part in the cosmic All-life more and more. These garments limit the ether body's capacity to act, which means that they restrict the soul. Through the continuous violation of the divine laws, these seven envelopments, the basic garments of the soul, became more and more condensed. The result was that the soul became smaller and its seven times seven pure paths of life were led closer and closer to the central point, to the "heart" of the spirit being. These seven shaded basic garments now form the crystallized shape outside the soul mass. The most strongly crystallized ether is called human being.

When the shape of the human being, that is, the highest degree of condensation of the ether, had formed for the most part, the seven basic garments of the soul in the human body contracted to become spiritually compressed points, which are now called consciousness centers. These seven basic garments of the soul, or the seven consciousness centers in the physical body, must be dissolved again one day through a corresponding way of life by the human being or by the soul in the purification planes, so that the soul can again enter the eternally existing infinity as a pure ether form.

Only once these spiritual consciousness centers become more strongly active in the human being, will increased ether powers flow into the body via the soul, which bring the cells into a high vibration, thus giving them increased spiritual energy. Through this energy, the vital power is lawfully increased. In this way, the human being also receives the right spiritual connection to God and to creation. These ether powers that flow into the human being via the consciousness centers, and through the spiritual supply veins, then enlarge the constricted and reduced soul-mass. As a result, the human consciousness expands, and the human being perceives and reacts more consciously and finely than the sleeping and strongly diminished soul, which conveys the ether powers to its body only drop by drop.

What is a spiritual vegetarian?

A spiritually oriented vegetarian not only strives for a healthy way of life which, for instance, is based on organic grains, fruits and vegetables, but lives more from the ether power. A spiritual vegetarian is a sensitive person, who is guided and directed by the ether powers, that is, by God, our Lord. He recognizes the ruling Spirit in all life forms and knows that He is the origin and the preserver of both the soul and the physical body.

The unknowing human being reaches for herbs, and if they do not become effective immediately, he reaches for pills. The person who is oriented to matter alone immediately reaches for medication.

However, the knowing person, before he takes herbs or even medicine, links with the Inner Physician and Healer, with the eternally existing ether power, which flows differently in every human being. According to the soul's activity and its degree of purity, the physical body, too, receives ether powers. They provide the actual sustenance for the soul and mostly for the human being, too, if he leads a lawful life. These ether powers also relieve and heal; they reduce agitation and ignoble inclinations; they transform sensuality into the joy of a pure life in God and let the human being become a virtuous child of God.

Conduct with headaches
Possible causes of this complaint

The spiritual vegetarian who turns to the ether powers, to God, acts in a certain manner in case of illness:

Let us take a headache as an example, however it was caused.

A headache can be more or less intense and can often get out of hand and become a severe migraine. Every headache, no matter how strong it may be, has its cause: either in the soul or in the body. The cause of a headache can be, for instance, a weak or sick organ of the body, or overstrained nerves, weariness or unlawful food. But also changes in blood circulation or of the heart function, of glands and hormones can cause headaches. The human being cannot immediately analyze the cause.

The spiritual vegetarian, the spiritual human being who puts his hope in God and trusts Him, aligns more with the inner source, the ether powers, with the Inner Physician and Healer. This inner power gives the inwardly oriented person the proper medication, the ether power, in the exact dose needed. The person who is aligned with God knows that the Inner

Physician and Healer can become active and help at any time to dissolve the pain and to give the body vitality again. A spiritual vegetarian will briefly think about what the reason might be for the headache: "What did I eat? How did I prepare the meal? Was I upset? Did I act thoughtlessly? Was I worried? Did I give off too much energy by talking about unessential things? Did I think or act negatively? How did I treat my fellowman during the past days? Was I restless? What was I thinking? Did I occupy myself with unessential things, which robbed my energy of life and strained my nerves?" The spiritual vegetarian knows that a headache mostly points to an energy block in the body. For this reason, he makes a brief self-analysis and then, he often recognizes the reason for the headache.

How does he conduct himself? Was his headache caused by nervous tension, which is often caused by unpleasant conversations, too much pondering, or even by insufficient sleep? If so, he darkens the room if possible, and lies down flat on the floor, wrapping himself in a warm blanket, preferably made of natural fibers. He covers his head and eyes with a cloth, also made of natural fibers, preferably wool, or better yet, angora wool. The patient lies on his back, both arms on the floor, with palms facing upward and his legs propped up just a little at the knees. The eyes are closed. Now he tries to let go of all worldly thoughts. He directs his thoughts toward the sixth consciousness center, which is located between the eyes, and asks the eternal Spirit for life force and relaxation. Then he watches his breathing, that is, he lets "It" breathe, inhaling through the nose and exhaling through the mouth. In this way, no artificial inhalation and exhalation result, but a very natural, rhythmic breathing. The one seeking healing is aware that healing and relaxing powers are flowing into him via his breath.

Through the power of thought, which rests in the sixth consciousness center, the ether powers are requested from the core of being in the soul, the seat of the Godhead. These spiritual powers then begin to slowly flow into the soul and, via the invoked consciousness center, into the human being. The warming blanket, made of natural fibers, and the corresponding head covering additionally contribute to relaxation. The body becomes warm and thus, the cells and nerves relax. At the same time, the high vibrations of the natural fibers connect with the now more intensely flowing ether powers and let the healing streams flow inside and outside the body. In this way, the body is magnetized and charged with Spirit power. Through this spiritual therapy, very tense organs, which may have contributed to the headache, can often relax.

For these exercises to be done successfully, first of all, faith in God and in the inner healing power is necessary. Here, too, as with everything asked of the Spirit, the person has to be patient. As revealed before, the ether powers must first be activated by a corresponding life, before they can become effective from one minute to the next. Bear in mind, O human being, that you cannot build your earthly house from one day to the next and you cannot move into it from today to tomorrow. Even moving into your new house often takes several weeks or even months.

Think in a likewise manner when you are in pain, and the Spirit cannot help you immediately. Ask yourself: "Is my body a pure temple of the Holy Spirit? How did I treat this physical house over the course of my life on Earth, and how did I maintain it? Has this house of flesh and bone become unsound and derelict, because I rarely cleaned and repaired it? Was it built only with the building blocks of this world, through which only the power of human thinking and acting is flowing, or have I purified and built up my temple through a corresponding divine way of life, so that the inner powers, the eternally existing ether powers, can immediately become effective?"

If the human being did not purify his body by turning toward God, and through a corresponding diet, and his body consequently became weary and tormented by illnesses, then remember, O human being, that the ether powers within you are effective only in a small way, because you did not give them the possibility to unfold during your life on Earth. Therefore, you cannot expect the divine ether powers to flow in their full extent into your derelict house and immediately restore it, from one day to the next.

Therefore, be patient and purify your temple from the rubbish of this world, by putting order in your life; this means, above all in your thoughts and actions, but also by thinking about your eating habits. And include the question: "How did I act and how do I still act toward the kingdom of nature?" Recognize, O human being, that your soul is the essence of creation and therefore, the mineral, plant, and animal kingdoms are respective building blocks of your soul. Endeavor to treat them accordingly!

Contingent upon your age, your house will eventually become dilapidated, but you will not have any all too great complaints, since the holy ether powers keep your temple fresh and healthy for a long time.

When you are lying on the floor and you want to rid yourself of your headache with the help of the ether powers, then, as already advised, first let your thoughts rest in God and stay with the sixth consciousness center in your sensations. The healing streams flow into your organism by way of this energy point. All seven consciousness centers in the body are linked by the ether channels. They are the distribution points for the inflowing ether powers. Every organ of the physical body is connected with one of these power centers and receives the energy necessary for life in this way. The brain, for instance, is supplied with the holy ether power via the sixth consciousness center. By turning your thoughts to the divine powers in this sixth consciousness center, increased ether powers flow from there to the tense cells of the brain.

If you suffer from a headache, then remain in this relaxed position for approximately 15 minutes; concentrate your sensations solely on the sixth consciousness center, and know that God, the Inner Physician and Healer, the ether power, is in you. If you should fall asleep in the meantime, this is also good. Through the relaxation of the body and the warmth, the person often falls into a deep, restful sleep.

Once you awaken, or once you can move without pain again after about 15 minutes, do not allow your thoughts to run free again. Continue to align them with God, thus combating the causes for your illness.

Go to an open window; breathe in fresh, but not cold, air. Then let cold, but not ice cold, water flow down your arms, starting from the elbows.

Then put on warm clothing, because a body that is kept warm relaxes and heals.

If you are now hungry, eat only easily digested foods. Prepare them calmly. Do not eat heavy bread right away, but perhaps fruit or quickly digested, non-flatulent vegetables.

If necessary, you can also drink a cup of relaxing herbal tea. Do not drink it too hot, please, only good and warm, and drink it in sips. There are several different herbs that lead to even more relaxation and relief, for instance – lesser centaury, balm mint (also called lemon balm), lavender and St. John's Wort, or one or two sips of wormwood tea. Please, do not drink a full cup of wormwood tea, only one or two sips!

These revelations come from the Spirit of God and are meant to be spiritual aids for our brothers and sisters. If they are applied correctly and practiced in life, they are of the highest spiritual value, not only for the body, but also for the soul. However, the Spirit does not dissuade you from consulting a doctor in the world.

May the one seeking healing understand that the spiritual healing methods can be effective only when the human being turns to the Inner Physician and Healer in total faith and confidence, when he recognizes his faults and weaknesses and analyzes his life. The divine powers will become fully effective in the soul and person only after he leads a life in the will of God and can thus call on the Inner Physician and Healer at any time. This revealed knowledge is a gift of grace and a help for those who have trained their trust in God and also actualize the law of the Lord for the most part.

However, if the headache should *not* go away and you still feel weak and bothered by pain, then, think over again the possible reasons for your pain.

Now you will reach for medicine. However, let this not be your only help, but rather, do think over what you could do better in the future, in your life, in your thinking and doing, so that without medicine you can defeat a headache that may come up again later.

Bless the medicine in the name of the Lord before you take it, so that the holy power, which rests in the thought of blessing, largely absorbs the harmful substances in the medicine. Through the request for blessing, the ether powers flowing through the medicine become more effective.

Headaches can also have many physical reasons: over-fatigue of the eyes, poor vision, excessive intake of medicine for other ailments, excessive and fatty meals, constant burdening of the intestines, metabolic disorders, flatulence and a feeling of abdominal fullness.

Therefore, O human being, think about what you eat and how you eat it. Do you gulp down your food, without chewing it consciously? Examine your body's posture and your movements as well: A poor posture and every hectic movement contribute to a possible illness of your body. All these are causes that show their effects sooner or later.

Uncontrolled lust for eating indicates uncontrolled sensuality. Sensuality is also aroused by corresponding sensations and thoughts, indeed, also by low-vibrating food and the like. Sensuality also contributes to the tension of the nervous system and to the body falling ill. You will not become healthy by relaxing through sensuality alone, because your body loses valuable bearers of life through this.

Therefore, the person should bring this emotional hunger for life to God, as well, so that these arousals can be transformed into spiritual activity. If you think that this loss of strength can be compensated for by food, you are mistaken. If this loss of strength can no longer be felt in this life, then certainly in the next life on this Earth or by the soul in the soul realms.

*Relief of tension
and pain through meditation*

If the person who suffers from a headache cannot lie flat on the floor in order to follow the previously given instructions, then he may sit upright for a short time, that is, take up the Christian meditation posture. This is done as follows: Place both feet on the floor, sit upright, hold your head straight, place the back of your hands on your thighs and close your eyes. Thereupon, say a short prayer request and free yourself totally of troublesome thoughts. Surrender all your thoughts to the Christ-power, which is active in the fourth consciousness center in your chest.

Provided you cannot yet concentrate on this Christ-light, then first push all base inclinations and thoughts, which make you restless and bring a lack of peace, away from you and see them as a picture that forms *outside* of your own self. Briefly watch this thought-picture, which formed outside of you, and analyze what troubles and oppresses you. In this calm posture – from a higher perspective – examine whether the occurrences captured in the picture are worth, perhaps, becoming so upset and tense, that you are now bothered by a headache or even a migraine. In this quiet meditation posture, a person often recognizes that many things are not as serious as he felt in his inner being. Only when a person gains this recognition will he become calm and relaxed.

Thus, if you notice that your situation is not so serious, first breathe in and out deeply several times. Again, like a critical painter, now look at this thought-picture, of which some parts are still there, and touch up everything that is not essential, and surrender it to the consuming flame that is waiting to redeem and liberate your soul.

But also surrender to the Christ-light the important facts that remained in your thought-picture, and ask the Spirit of Christ for the solution to your still existing problems. Believe firmly in this helping hand and then free yourself completely from these impressions. Do not bring back these problems anymore, by thinking about them. As soon as you are preoccupied with them again, you draw them into your inner being; this means that your nerves register these returning thoughts, causing your brain and body cells to become tense again.

The causes of illness, indisposition, blows of fate and worries develop through an unlawful way of thinking and acting.

Once you have freed yourself from these unsettling thought-pictures, direct your sensations either to the fourth consciousness center, where the Christ-light is, the liberation of your earthly life, or to the central point of love, which is between your eyes. Both centers are highly vibrating, pulsating and rotating powers. The outpouring of the holy Spirit powers takes place via these two centers, as well as all other consciousness centers. Therefore, align with one of these two consciousness centers and try not to think of anything else.

As soon as thoughts rise up, send them away from you, and, in your sensations, hold on to one of these two points of power. Breathe deeply and consciously in and out a few more times and then let "It" breathe in you. Remain in this meditation posture as long as possible, at least ten minutes. The normal duration for this exercise is twenty to forty-five minutes. After this meditation of power, let water flow down your arms and hands, as already described, and slowly and consciously eat an apple, for instance, which you should chew thoroughly.

If you cannot immediately reach this meditative calmness, drink a relaxing tea first, maybe two or three sips of wormwood tea or a cup of calendula or St. John's Wort tea. These herbs can be mixed with silverweed. This time, drink this tea quite warm.

Basically, the Spirit recommends that when you feel physical and mental relief, it is very important to remain in this relaxed frame of mind without any thoughts. Do not try to resume the thought-picture which you have surrendered, and do not preoccupy yourself with it. Entrust yourself entirely to the guidance of God.

Patience and persistent devotion to God are decisive for success

In this book, I, spirit teacher Brother Emanuel, want to stress again and again that the ether powers, the Spirit powers of God, cannot become instantly effective, if up to now, the human being has not led an exemplary life in his earthly existence.

Often it is a karma, a soul-burden that wants to dissolve in the body. Provided the core of being in the soul, the central point of your cosmic life, becomes active, it pushes away all that is negative from it – and thus, out of the soul. Thus, these disharmonies flow into your body and touch the respective organs. Therefore, do not complain and do not accuse God for the guilt of the soul that you have created yourself, because everything that becomes apparent in your body is based on cause and effect. God is a God of perfection. He, the Lord, created only perfection. Any imperfection is based on a human way of thinking and acting.

Therefore, O human being, be patient with yourself, just as God is patient with you and try to constantly devote yourself to Him, who is the perfect life. The eternally existing divine power will certainly bring you the desired success at the right time, according to the law of God. Jesus essentially said: "Your sins are forgiven, go and sin no more." Or: "It is given to you according to your faith."

If a person wants to turn to the Inner Physician and Healer, it is decisive that he change his life, that is, his way of thinking and acting. By turning to the all-existing power, the person will draw daily more and more ether powers from the wellspring of divine life.

I, Brother Emanuel, must point out very clearly and firmly that the Spirit of God does not dissuade anyone from consulting a doctor in the world, because the effectiveness of the conduct recommended in these divine revelations depends entirely on the human being himself, how he devotes himself to God, and how he thinks and acts in his daily life.

However, it is often possible for the Inner Physician and Healer to help His child immediately, through an ether channel that has already opened somewhat wider, that is, provided the illness can be touched via this particular ether channel. Every organ is supplied with spiritual power-streams via one of the seven consciousness centers. Therefore, if a consciousness channel is somewhat more open, ether powers can increasingly flow into the respective organs by way of said channel. In this way, the patient often experiences immediate relief or healing.

It is therefore advisable that a person not devote himself to God only when he falls ill or when need forces him to, but consistently in his daily life. At every moment, a person should be in conscious contact with God, His Lord! The inner Helper can become effective much more quickly in a person who is continuously turned to the divine.

Once the help through grace has become effective and improvement or even healing are experienced, the human being often falls back into his old habits. By acting against the divine law, the old illnesses can appear again, sooner or later.

What is absolutely decisive is the lasting devotion to God, so that the eternally existing ether powers can become and remain effective. The great Physician and Healer, the law of God in the human being, is omniscient and omnipresent. This eternal power of love wants to soothe, heal, help and give peace. God is only waiting to help His child. Therefore, O human being, prove yourself to be a vessel of God and not an instrument of this world.

The human being should consciously turn to the strengthening ether powers early in the morning

The sun rises in the east.

During sunrise, but also several times during the day, a person should turn east with his hands raised. This should be done especially in the early morning hours.

When a part of the Earth enters the night, increased ether powers spread over it from the eternal spheres, mainly pouring out over the kingdoms of minerals and plants. Mighty ether waves rise and touch everything that turns to them. These invisible ether waves penetrate all bodies and forms that open themselves to them. Therefore, it is especially beneficial to give oneself to these ether waves during the morning hours.

Mentally disturbed people, too, are advised to turn their body toward the east during the early morning hours, if possible, with raised hands, that is, face and palms should be turned toward the east. These powers put many things in order in the body; they stimulate the cells and can often influence weaknesses and damages in the brain and tumors in a very positive way. Hearing problems as well as disorders of the tonsils and adenoids and of the heart can be beneficially touched by ether powers flowing in from the east.

The flowing ether powers can be felt as beneficial and refreshing, especially in the Christian meditation posture and particularly in the early morning hours. The absorption of the ether powers leads to a stabilization of the whole body. Someone who absorbs them consciously and knows how to guide them through the power of thought, and according to the law of God, will feel these life forces after only a short time.

The healing ether powers in dew

During the summer months, when dew covers the meadows, people with a weak heart, circulatory problems, narrowing of the veins, calcification of blood vessels and metabolic disorders should alternately walk on dew and rub themselves with it. People with weak eyes, cataracts and glaucoma should put the morning dew on their eyes. The leaves of walnut trees or of coltsfoot, and large plantain leaves attract ether powers to a high degree and, therefore, have dew with especially high strengthening qualities. These leaves with the dew on them, can be put on the eyes or on badly healing wounds. A piece of muslin should be placed on the wound first.

People suffering from migraine-like headaches can also make use of the morning dew by rubbing it on the forehead, temples and neck. Walking on dew is also very essential for them. Seekers of healing with very weak nerves should rub the whole body with dew several times a week, because in the dew there are highly vibrating ether powers that want to serve the human being.

For rashes on the body that were caused by unclean things, the dew of the stinging nettle should be used in the morning hours. Put on a linen glove and rub it over the stinging nettle; then rub the whole body with this dew. And, conscious breathing before a big field of stinging nettles stabilizes blood circulation and gives blood vitalizing, purifying substances.

Facial erysipelas can also be treated successfully with morning dew.

Walking on dew during spring, shortly before sunrise, strengthens the circulation and has a vitalizing effect.

The following can be recommended if you suffer from rheumatism or gout: Rub the whole body with dew, or – if possible – wrap yourself in a porous cloth and lie down in the stinging nettles during the early morning hours. This helps to soothe and heal rheumatism. This is also helpful for people susceptible to rickets. Gout, too, can be relieved or healed in this way.

After the body has been rubbed with morning dew, it should be dressed warmly, not with synthetic fibers, but clothing made of natural fibers. It is also very important – especially after walking on dew – to keep the feet warm. Put on warm woolen stockings reaching over the knees. The knees, too, should always be protected.

Concerning all that I advise and reveal here, it has to be mentioned again and again: These healing methods are based exclusively on the divine laws and become effective only when the human being turns to the Spirit of God, the law.

If the one seeking healing decides to totally give himself to the law of God, to the eternally existing ether powers, he must bear in mind that if he is taking medications he cannot stop taking them from one day to the next. This would be a mistake because, first of all, the devotion to the law of God in faith and trust is necessary, and above all, its fulfillment. If a person is truly serious about this, he should very slowly withdraw the amount of medicine he is taking. I recommend herbal remedies as a support and transition. Please do not resort to the use of "forceful" applications. This would not lead to the outpouring of the ether powers. On the contrary, the body's condition could become even worse in several respects.

The alignment with the magnetic currents of the Earth – A support for the sick or weak organism

An alignment with the magnetic currents, about which I will give a detailed revelation, is also a good support and help for the human being who has not yet spiritually awakened and is not yet filled with light by the Spirit of God. Even though the Earth's magnetic currents are considerably disturbed by negative sources and by the negative actions of human beings, nevertheless, they have a positive effect on some people, provided their energy field is very weak and cannot really stimulate and straighten the body. As with many other realizations, the following holds true: The negative aspect of a force can strengthen the positive.

Thus, magnetic currents are often very beneficial for weak, tired and sickly people. They magnetize the entire organism, build up weak cells again, regulate the circulation and stabilize the nerves. Also, for mentally weak and ill people, as well as epileptics, the magnetic currents are strengthening and vitalizing.

For symptoms of fatigue, which often appear around noontime, the following advice can be given: At this time, the sun is at its highest position. If the first symptoms of fatigue appear, caused by daily activity, the knowing person who would like to recover should not go to any random place. Only an unknowing, worldly person does this. The knowing person, however, pays attention to his position or his posture. In case he reacts to water veins, he should also take care that he does not sit or lie on a water vein, or even on a crossing of water veins, because they make the body restless and bring no relaxation or recovery.

An uninstructed person believes that a short rest and a cup of coffee will give him back the necessary energy so that he can go on working dynamically.

Unless karmic causes exist, tumors, dizziness, exhaustion, nervousness, mental disorder, epileptic seizures, migraines, heart trouble, narrowing of the veins and inflammation can often be the result of a wrongly chosen position of rest for the body, made out of ignorance.

I now give some directions concerning this, which, however, are only for those people who do not yet feel the activity of the ether powers in themselves. They are not necessary for those people who keep the divine laws and continuously remember the eternal and holy powers, asking for them daily. The active and highly vibrating ether powers in them can keep any danger away from the physical body, because they absorb the penetrating, low-vibrating radiation, so that it cannot become effective in the body.

If the ether powers are not yet active in them, tired, sickly people, or those who suffer from the illnesses mentioned above or similar ones, should make use of the magnetic currents and, additionally, the ether powers coming from the east. And those people who frequently allow themselves periods of rest should consider these external aids which, as already revealed, apply only until the Inner Physician and Healer becomes effective. Only when the inner

Spirit powers come into play will the external aids become secondary.

Thus, if you want to make use of magnetic currents, lie flat on the floor. Lying flat without a pillow is mainly for people who have no eye or head impairments. If possible, lie on the floor, so that the body is stretched out. The top of your head should point to the north. The hands should rest on the ground, palms turned upward. Now pull both legs to the body and place your feet – without shoes – on the floor. Then breathe deeply in and out several times; while doing so, empty yourself of all burdening thoughts. As a support, you can concentrate again on the sixth consciousness center between your eyes. Stay with it in your sensations. Close your eyes and let "It" breathe. If it is difficult for you to concentrate on the sixth center, then watch how your breath comes and goes smoothly, and how you become calmer, provided you were able to free yourself from burdening thoughts. Remain in this position for at least ten minutes.

After this rest, rise slowly and continue your work. Remain calm and quiet. Do not think right away that the exercise was of no use. Do not watch yourself, but believe in the invoked powers, so that they can become effective by your constant orientation to them.

Through a Christian meditation posture, in which body and face are turned to the north, the magnetic currents of the Earth can charge the body's magnetic field as well as the cell structure. In this way, strength is collected and activated. On the other hand, if the one seeking healing wants to absorb the ether powers that flow mainly from the east, especially during the early morning hours, he should face east in the meditation posture.

Beneficial effects of water veins and the crossing of water veins

Mentally disturbed people, epileptics and people with tumors, however, should lie down on water veins, but only on those that flow from the north. They have a high radiation of silver, manganese, copper, and also a certain amount of lead radiation. Especially these vibrational forces contribute to the activation of certain cells in the cerebrum and cerebellum.

Individuals with poor digestion thoughtlessly reach for medicine. It could often be helpful if they would linger on certain harmless crossings of water veins. Such beneficial crossings are located where there is a swarm of gnats dancing, for instance. By lingering on such a crossing, the body's magnetic field is strengthened and its metabolism activated.

On spots where there are big ant hills, there are also crossings of benign water veins. On these spots there are many vapors and vibrations of formic acid, which have a positive influence on the solar plexus and contribute to mental and physical activity. They also influence the blood count in a salutary way, and toughen the nerves.

In cases of cancer, it would also be good to affirm this procedure. However, to strongly unfold these lawful healing forces, a deep alignment of the one seeking healing with God, the all-permeating Spirit, is decisive. To linger in the divine consciousness on such spots leads to the absorption of these rising vibrations, which stabilize the person's magnetic field and strengthen his whole human structure.

*How can people who possess
special spiritual abilities,
for instance, dowsers, be tested?*

Many people have spiritual gifts. Dowsers, too, possess powers that can come from the Spirit of God. The Spirit of God gives His gifts abundantly, but only to those who turn to the Spirit of God. Therefore, above all, examine the person who possesses these spiritual gifts. Then, as it is written, draw conclusions about the spirits that guide the person. Ask how such an individual lives, thinks and speaks. From this, a spiritually mature person can recognize what kind of person is the one who possesses such and similar talents, and what being guides him.

If such a person speaks only of *his* talents and knowledge, and considers all others second or even third class, then be cautious. If a person considers himself to be more than others, and puts himself above others, then caution is called for. And if he takes money and gifts for his service to his neighbor, that is, if he accepts a remuneration for a spiritual gift, then likewise be cautious.

A human being devoted to God, who has received from God a talent that helps his neighbor, even when it comes to identifying water veins, can work for the benefit and welfare of all. Such a gifted human being can often detect subterranean sources of danger with his bare hands, provided he has received these gifts of grace exclusively from God, the Spirit of life. He can also detect mineral springs and healing currents that are beneficial for the physical body.

All the revelations that I give here in the name of the Lord are gifts of the Spirit, which benefit those who devote themselves more to the Spirit of God, and who trust Him more than the human spirit, also called the spirit of the times, on which only short-lived partial knowledge is based.

Healing meditation for brain tumors
and mental retardation
Pointers for the absorption of the
Earth's magnetic currents with brain injury,
epilepsy and the like

A person who has a brain tumor or is mentally retarded should cover his head, especially on cool days or very hot ones. However, for relieving and healing these diseases, as with all complaints, the *ether powers* should, above all, be invoked.

It is also essential that such seekers of healing are granted much rest and tranquility. Walks in the woods during morning hours, especially in areas where there are large forests, are also advisable. Likewise, a morning meditation for which the patient faces east while concentrating on the sixth consciousness center of divine love, which, as already revealed, is between the physical eyes, is advisable. In addition, everyone who practices such a healing meditation should know that the life forces that actively express themselves by way of the sixth consciousness center become effective only if he leads a life according to the law of God.

If a person turns to the east to receive the ether powers, it is of no importance what kind of building he is in. But if it is possible to meditate out in the open or in a wooden house, this can only be welcomed. However, if this is not possible, there is no objection to meditating in a house built of any other material. What is most important in absorbing the ether powers, which are divine powers, is a proper attitude and a way of life that is in alignment with God and according to the divine laws.

It is different when aligning with the Earth's magnetic currents.

Take care that your dwelling or the place for absorbing these magnetic currents is not situated on an approach path for airplanes. These currents are continuously disturbed in such areas.

Nor should you live under high-tension lines or over an electrical system or even lie down there to absorb the Earth's magnetic currents. In such areas, a person achieves rather the opposite.

These energies influence and continuously disturb the Earth's magnetic currents. Through this, the magnetic field of your body will also be impaired, which can lead to injuries of the nerves and of the body. Such and similar burdening of the body can also result in mental distress.

Those seeking healing, who are suffering from a brain tumor, epilepsy or brain damage are advised to activate the ether powers in the sixth consciousness center, as already revealed. By way of this power potential of the Spirit, the brain cells are also nourished, and the disturbing factors there are eliminated.

Moreover, these patients should not disregard the magnetic currents that flow more intensely and deliver higher energies especially around noontime. However, the magnetizing of the body is, like everything that comes from without, merely a support for the physical body. The eternally powerful and lasting elixir of life is *in* the person, himself. It is the Inner Physician and Healer, the eternally flowing ether power.

To absorb the Earth's magnetic currents, the one seeking healing should, at best, lie on the floor. However, if he suffers from a brain tumor or any other severe brain injury, he should never lie totally flat. The same holds true for epilepsy, although here, it depends totally on the degree of the disorder. For severe eye diseases, the patient should, perhaps, also use a pillow that is not too thick. Each one must try out for himself what is best for him. During the summer months, it is advisable to absorb the Earth's magnetic currents as well as the ether powers outdoors – if it is very hot, then, in the shade.

Invocation of the ether powers with headaches, migraine and brain disorders

For healing or soothing the three kinds of ailments just mentioned above, as well as for headaches and migraine, the ether power should be invoked in the sixth consciousness center as follows:

"O Lord, Your will be done in me.
I open myself only to Your powers. They shall become active in me *according to Your will* and shall remove the illnesses or weaknesses."

Then, via your sensations, guide the divine energy of the sixth consciousness center to the ill or painful parts in your head.

The recommended affirmation expressing devotion and faith is essential. But it should not be said in a shallow manner. A strong intention must be behind it and the child must fully surrender to the will of the divine Spirit. This has the following significance:

*The surrender solely to the will
of God is necessary – Dangers
involved with invoking the Spirit power*

Through this "bridge of trust" to God, our Lord, negative streams, which also flow from souls in the astral spheres (purification planes) and could possibly gain access, are eliminated.

If the human being merely invokes the Spirit power and does not open the channel to the power of God – by devoting himself exclusively to the Spirit of God, the great Physician and Healer, in the request: "Lord, only Your will be done" – he can open a channel to the spheres of the beyond. From there, possible healing influences from souls who were physicians in previous lives on Earth can reach the body and disturb it. Through various channels, these unknowing souls can also take energy from other people and from animals and lead it to people who are hoping for healing.

In this way, a healing can take place, here and there, but a possibly existing burden of the soul, a karma, is not considered in the process. The person may very well become healthy in this life. The soul, however, remains sick and must take its outflowing karma into a further life on Earth. The burden of the soul can then become apparent in a greater and more extensive way than in the present life, because through an uncontrolled life many additional things have accumulated, which then also come into effect.

The same can happen if the human being entrusts himself to spirit healers who are not under the grace of Christ. I do not want to go into detail about this here.

*Illnesses in your head can be
relieved or healed by activating the
sixth consciousness center*

If you have not yet learned to guide the divine ether powers, then devote yourself to God. As advised, ask for His Spirit power, and direct your attention to the sixth consciousness center, the center of Love. As with all consciousness centers, this sixth consciousness center can be understood as a radiant energy field that rotates as in a spiral movement.

The concept of this pulsating and simultaneously rotating "wheel of consciousness" should merely be a point of reference for the spiritually untrained person. The spiritually knowing person recognizes this wheel as a power of God of differing intensity and nuance of color, depending on the mental-spiritual maturity of a person. This wheel of consciousness consists of ether streams. The more the human being surrenders himself to God and prays to God for salvation, and also proves himself in his life by applying the divine laws, the more each one of these seven consciousness wheels, but, above all, the sixth, becomes active.

The following organs of the body are connected to this sixth consciousness center: cerebrum, cerebellum, with the pituitary gland and pineal gland, ears, nose and eyes.

If you have not yet mastered the art of directing the divine ether streams, you can confidently place into this sixth consciousness center your headaches, migraines, mental retardation, brain disorders, brain tumors, epileptic seizures, your eye disorders and defective vision, as well as the disorders of your nose, tonsils and ears, and the impairments of your spinal column, nervous debility, insomnia and depression. In addition, you can place into this center of Love all other disorders whose origin is unknown to you.

This sixth center is – as is the fourth wheel of consciousness, where the Christ-center, the Redeemer-light is located – a control center for the ether powers, which are distributed from there to all organs and cells of the body via the ether channels.

However, it is better and more precise if you directly invoke the consciousness center with which the diseased organ of the body is connected via the ether channels. I shall give the necessary instructions for this during the course of this revelation. The ether powers that have been activated in such a way can reach the diseased organs more quickly. Thus, the power centers of the ether tree are the distribution points of the divine Spirit powers. Provided these consciousness centers are correctly invoked, the ether powers flow – via certain spiritual supply channels – to those organs that receive their life energy through these channels.

This means that through the power of his thoughts, the knowing person can activate the divine healing forces in himself and apply them for his recovery. Provided his thoughts are based on the law of God, high ether powers are set free that serve the person and all life forms. Thus, the ether powers can be requested via specific centers, through which they become effective in the diseased and weak organs within a short time.

At this point, I must mention again: These revelations are given from the Spirit of God.

The ether powers can become fully effective only if the person surrenders to these forces and does not merely ask for them, but also leads a spiritually consistent life. Should the requested powers not become effective and not bring the desired result, then may the person examine the degree of his devotion to God and his way of life as well, and not think that these divine healing powers do not exist.

Prerequisites for the effectiveness of the healing ether powers in a person

The divine ether powers are the holy law, which permeates all life forms, including human beings. The eternal ether powers are the fount of health of all creation. They flow constantly and refresh all those people and souls who turn to the law of God.

These ether powers flow via the consciousness centers into the cell structure of the physical body.

The more purified the soul of a human being is, the more strongly these holy powers flow into the human body.

The ether powers in a human being are the Inner Physician and Healer, which every person can invoke. If a person turns to Him in a lawful way and leads a corresponding life, this Inner Physician goes to work immediately and becomes active in the cell children. God, the Lord, the ether power in the person, is willing to help the child and to serve him at any time.

Since humankind moves further and further away from God, its Lord, it is not always possible for God, the Spirit of life, to support His children immediately. Because of his impure life, the human being does not know how to invoke the ether powers, and even pushes them away, by way of his spiritual-physical burdens. Therefore, the soul and the seven power centers in the person are often reversed in their polarity for the most part. This is why the healing and helping ether powers cannot become effective immediately.

For this reason, if the person now wants to turn to the great Physician and Healer, the ether powers, he should be patient with himself. Because it was he who neglected these holy powers through an impure way of life.

The ether tree in the human being supplies all the organs of the body with the holy ether power – Significance of the seven consciousness centers

The ether channels in human beings are arranged like a tree. The seven consciousness centers form the trunk of this ether tree. Seven ether channels go out from each of these seven powers. They penetrate the particular organs of the physical body, each of which is connected to one consciousness center.

As soon as the soul leaves its physical body, it draws these seven energy fields back into itself and forms seven garments from them. These seven garments then envelop the eternal ether body with its core of being. As long as these seven garments exist, the eternal ether body is called soul. Only once these seven garments have again dissolved, by way of the purification and cleansing of the soul, can the ether body return to the pure heavens, which it once left through the Fall.

As long as the soul is in the body – it is located near the pituitary gland – the following applies: The lighter, that is, the more flexible, a wheel of consciousness is, the more ether powers flow into the body of the human being. It is therefore possible for the person to ask for the healing Spirit power for his organs via these consciousness centers.

These life forces, the ether powers, flow in the ethereal tree of life in the person, down the left side of the spinal column. In doing so, they already touch the seven consciousness centers and give the body vitality and well-being even while flowing down. These life forces collect in the pelvis and are then drawn up to itself by the power of the fourth consciousness center, the center of Earnestness, in which the Spirit of Christ, the Redeemer-light, is effective.

From there, they are forwarded – likewise via the power of the fourth center – to the fifth and sixth consciousness centers, namely, in the second ether channel, which runs along the right side of the spinal column. The sixth consciousness center contains, just as the fourth center of power, a high source of energy, which, at the same time, rotates and pulsates within itself more intensely than all other consciousness centers. Through the power of this sixth center, the rising ether powers in the second ether channel on the right side of the spinal column are forwarded to the seventh consciousness center, the gate to the Absoluteness. From there, the core of being of the soul, the *eternal* God-Spark, draws these ether powers to itself.

Starting with the core of being of the soul, the spiritual ether circulation begins anew. The more a person devotes himself to God, his Father, and prays from his heart with faith and confidence and is selflessly active for his fellowman according to the divine commandment, the more intensely and quickly flows this spiritual circulation of energy.

Provided this ether circulation is in increased action, the human being is largely healthy and filled with vitality.

The human being should also be informed about his spiritual ether circulation, so that through a lawful life he can activate this most important circulation effective in him. Then, he can invoke the necessary healing powers for his sick cells, organs, glands and hormones via the consciousness centers – as explained in this book.

Essentially, it is written: "Ask and it will be given to you, seek and you will find, knock and the door will be opened to you." Generally speaking, this means: Lead a life according to the will of God, so that God can answer your requests – which are in accordance with the law – via one of the seven consciousness centers in your body.

The following organs are connected to the fifth consciousness center: tonsils, thyroid gland, larynx, throat, teeth and lungs. From the fifth consciousness center, the ether powers flow partly into the area of the nose, as well, in order to vitalize the cell structure there that leads to the throat area. The upper respiratory tract can also be addressed via the fifth center.

Thus, this means that via the fifth field of energy, we invoke the ether powers for all those organs that are located near this fifth center, that is, in the neck region.

It is written: "Ask and it will be given to you."

Many brothers and sisters will say: "It is enough to pray. God, our Lord, knows what I lack." Basically, this is correct. But a person should know not only his physical body, but also his ether body and its function. Sooner or later, that is, as soon as the soul has left its physical house, it must learn how to deal with its ether body. This ether body comes into action only by way of its seven energy fields, which form its basic powers. Through their complete development, that is, activation, the ether body finally becomes one with the entire spiritual universe, thus, gaining harmony with the Infinite.

Therefore, the one who, while still a human being, is informed about the existence of his spiritual body and its function can not only vitalize the elemental powers of his soul, but also keep his physical body active via these powers. This only requires a conscious addressing of the consciousness centers.

Just as every organ in the body has its function and is an indispensable little wheel in the entire organism, which should be healthy and functioning according to the body's rhythms, so should the wheels of consciousness also move according to the cosmic rhythm. Then, the physical body could also be sufficiently supplied with cosmic energy.

Each of these spiritual energy fields corresponds to an ethical-moral level of the law, which is, at the same time, an evolutionary level of the soul. If a human being violates one of these lawful principles, that is, one of these energy fields, he hinders the ether flow in this consciousness center. In the same way, the supply of ether energy to the organs of the body that are directly or indirectly connected to this consciousness center is reduced. Over the course of time, this leads to a weakening, and finally, to a disorder of one or several organs.

I want to briefly explain these seven centers, starting from the top of the head.

The highest consciousness center, the seventh one, is the gate to Absoluteness. It is called the center of Mercy. If this center is fully active, then all other six energy fields in the body are absolutely purified. Via this center, the first ether powers flow into the other consciousness centers, and from there – like the sap in a tree – they flow into the human body. For this reason, I begin by describing the consciousness centers starting from the top.

The folded-up, that is, encased soul, which is located near the pituitary gland, is the root of this tree of life in the human being. In it is the taproot leading to the core of being of God, the divine spark in the innermost part of the soul. By way of this taproot, all ether channels are supplied both in the soul and in the physical body.

The seventh consciousness center of Mercy, the gate to the soul, opens in accordance with the person's way of life.

The sixth center, the consciousness center of Love, which is located between the physical eyes, is an intensely rotating and pulsating source of energy. This center passes on the inflowing ether powers to the fifth consciousness center of Patience, in the area of the neck. Via the fifth center, the ether powers flow into the fourth center of Earnestness, which is located between the shoulder blades, near the heart. In this center, the Christ-light is active for all those who have not yet fully activated this consciousness center and all the centers below it.

From there, the ether powers flow, level by level, into the third center of divine Wisdom (lumbar area), into the second consciousness center of Will (area of the sacrum) and then into the lowest consciousness center of Order in the area of the coccyx.

The powers of each center act, in turn, as subregions in all other consciousness centers. This is why the human body is permeated by seven times seven ether channels. Through them, all organs and cells of the body are supplied with the life force, the ether, and are thus maintained and vivified.

Offenses against the divine laws diminish the flow of ether powers in the spiritual-physical circulation in the person. This results in a reduced level of consciousness and of healing possibilities. If a human being, as already described, violates one of these moral-energetic power fields, he reduces the flow of energy in the ether channels, which can then no longer supply the organs, cells, glands and hormones with life force to its full extent. This not only makes the healing possibility of the Inner Physician and Healer difficult, but the person's degree of enlightenment is also reduced. The soul's horizon in the person, his level of consciousness, is constricted.

The Spirit often states: "The revelations of heaven can be given to a person only according to his state of consciousness." This, in turn, means that the more the consciousness centers are reversed in their polarity, the lower is the person's mental and spiritual capacity. He has largely cut off the circulation in his soul. Therefore, no great interaction can take place between the ether power and the human being. The spiritual-divine capacity remains very minor, since the ether powers flow sparsely. This makes healing via the Christ-power very difficult.

Increased activity of the ether powers by way of self-analysis and refinement

Therefore, when a person asks the great Inner Physician and Healer for help, he should ask himself: "Which of the seven consciousness centers, that is, which of the ethical-moral principles that express themselves, have I mostly violated?" Once you have recognized yourself in self-analysis, ask for the grace of God in prayer. Over the course of time, this will change your life. This means that when a person changes toward what is lawful, the ether powers will increase their activity and will then, slowly but steadily, build up the consciousness centers and supply the physical body with life-giving forces.

For this reason, it is good if a person knows the function of his spirit body. In this way, he can recognize which consciousness center he is violating, and which heaven he has thus closed off to himself.

The one who knows about the reflecting arrangement of the heavenly regions in the soul and has learned to invoke the seven consciousness centers in his body has gained a great advantage for the spiritual evolution of his soul. By analyzing his life, his actions and their effects, he recognizes and knows which sphere of the law is not in a good state in his life. He can then invoke the consciousness center that has been reversed in its polarity through this, while simultaneously leading a better life in accordance with the will of God.

Jesus essentially said: "It is given to you according to your faith. Go and sin henceforth no more!" In a figurative sense, this means: Believe in God; recognize yourself; purify your soul by no longer sinning against the law of the Lord. Increased ether powers will then flow to you. On the other hand, if you fall back into your old habits, the old ailments will appear again as the ether powers diminish again. This is why the Lord added the sentence: "Go and sin henceforth no more!"

Healing meditation and healing exercises

The human being can devote himself to the Lord and induce the flow of the ether powers by praying in the following way:

My Lord and my God, my spirit rests in Your hands. I have inflicted many things on myself with my wrong way of thinking. And My actions did not always correspond with Your will.

Lord, I have recognized my faults and weaknesses for the most part. Please help me to discard them.

I am still weak in some things, and certainly I still have undetected shortcomings that my conscience was not yet able to show me, because I still see them as being good.

You, O Lord, are the Spirit of truth, love and justice. You shine through all Your children and recognize each of our weaknesses.
Help me to recognize these negative inclinations so that I can repent of them with all my heart, surrender them to You and improve myself.
You, great Spirit in me, know what is good for me and beneficial for my soul.

May only Your will be done.
I open the vessel of my soul for Your holy stream.
Your child wants to receive only Your wisdom, love and justice.

You can now assume an appropriate sitting or lying posture, either the Christian meditation position facing east, or if you wish to lie flat, with your head to the north. However, if it is only possible to assume a sitting position facing north, you can do this. To lie down would be more suitable, however. While lying down, put the backs of your hands on the floor, draw your legs up and place both feet flat on the floor. Now linger in total relaxation.

To entirely relax, inhale and exhale deeply several times.

An effective aid in relaxation is also to count through the seven consciousness centers going down and then back up again. This is done as follows:

Start with the seventh consciousness center, which is the gate to life, and which nestles very close to your soul. Visualize how, from there, the ether powers, the Spirit of God, flow into your body in a predetermined rhythm. Now, open this gate of consciousness in your thoughts and ask the Spirit for the increased flow of the ether powers into your physical body.

Breathe out slowly, thinking of this seventh consciousness center, and breathe slowly in again. While breathing in, leave the seventh wheel of consciousness in your sensations and concentrate on the sixth center. While inhaling, direct your full attention to this sixth center, the center of Love. Now exhale slowly and consciously again. Consciously means: Be aware that you are guiding the ether powers of the Lord according to His will. While doing this, remember that this is a holy act, and go to the fifth center with your sensations.
In the same way, breathe and count yourself down to the lowest center of power, which is located in the area of the coccyx.

The ether powers collect in the pelvis, below the first consciousness center. Tangibly relaxed, linger there for some time. Thereby, watch your breathing and think:

"The Spirit is breathing through my soul and my physical body. It is breathing in me and through me!"

Now breathe in and think of the lowest, the first, consciousness center. Recognize that now, the Christ-center draws up the ether powers that have flowed into the pelvis, to bring them to the consciousness centers lying above it. You now accompany the flow of the holy powers with a perfectly relaxed and easy breathing and by consciously thinking and counting upward:

You now breathe into the first center of power. With your sensations, you now accompany the ether powers to the second center. Having reached the second center, you breathe out slowly. You will now feel relief and vigor, for the spiritual circulation now comes into greater activity. Then slowly inhale again immediately, consciously, but completely relaxed and easy, and go one step higher while doing this, into the third consciousness center. While exhaling, go into the fourth center, then inhale immediately into the fifth center.

*Directions for activating the
fifth consciousness center
Toothache, festering tonsils, illnesses
of the respiratory organs*

If you want to ask for help, relief and healing by way of this fifth ether field, then remain in this ether field. Let "It" breathe. Then, activate this fifth consciousness center by praying somewhat like the following:

O Spirit, You, who are also active in my fifth consciousness center, I, Your child, ask You to stream through the cells connected with this power field. Activate and vivify them.
May new and strong cells form, while the sick ones are expelled by the power of the Spirit. O Lord of life, absorb them and transform them according to Your will, because in them, too, is still Your life.

If you have a toothache, for instance, now direct His ether powers to the painful area, fully relaxed and animated by the deep faith and confidence that the will of God will never forsake you.

Watch how everything in you expands and relaxes, how holy streams touch the cells, and how they accept this loving touch thankfully. Let everything be done in you, according to the divine will.

If relief from pain does not come immediately, do not be sad and in despair. Do not immediately discourage the activity of the cell children that were brought into action by the ether powers. Despite everything, be thankful, because you are still at the beginning of your understanding concerning the awakening of the cells.

If you are about to undergo dental treatment, then encourage your cells for this, as well. In this way, you will go to the dentist more light-heartedly and unconcerned. Recognize that the life is in every cell, which you can invoke and increasingly awaken with your highly vibrating sensations. If you send such highly vibrating sensations to your cell state, then the life in your cells will prepare themselves for the treatment to come; this means that the cells get ready for the potential procedure. They now send healing vibrations that loosen the tension in the cells.

When invoking the cells, use words like the following:

In every cell is the holy life, the ether power. I trustingly turn to this Inner Physician and Healer, and ask Him to send His warming and healing light to the cells concerned. I, too, the person, align totally with the Inner Physician and Healer, whom I trust implicitly and who will support me in all things.

If you have festering tonsils, direct the holy ether powers via the fifth field of power to the sick and swollen tonsils. Talk to these cells as you would to a sick child, because in every cell is the listening, divine life. Apologize to them and also to your blood circulation for not having cared properly for their well-being, so that through their illness, the blood circulation was also affected. Ultimately, an active blood circulation should transport these pathogens from your body. Now encourage your cell children by supplying them – lovingly, strongly believing and vivified by deep trust – with the ether powers that flow from the fifth consciousness center, knowing that God's will is able to do anything. Now, remain completely relaxed and let the holy ether powers, the Inner Physician and Healer, become effective in the cells. Feel how the cell mouths open and eagerly absorb the divine healing powers. Sense the holy and building up action of the eternal ether powers, and how sick and weak cells proceed to be eliminated. Now, feel your activated circulation, as well; it refreshes you and vivifies all organs and cells. Remain in stillness for a short time and let "It" take place in you.

If it is possible for you, these exercises should last approximately twenty minutes. You can repeat them twice a day. During the remaining time, in your daily life, try to remain balanced and harmonious and be aware of God's healing power in your body.

Via this fifth center you can activate – in a similar way as described here – the entire area of the throat and part of the upper respiratory passages. The lungs, too, can be partly addressed via this fifth center, because the ether channels, the branches that go out from this fifth power field, partly reach into your lungs. If you are suffering from bronchitis or disorders of your vocal chords, or of any organs that are near this fifth center, you may, O human being, invoke the fifth center according to the will of God.

Praise the cells of your body –
the life force in them will increase

Do not forget to consider that the cells are the building blocks of your body, that they live, and without a sufficient supply of ether energy, they can merely scrape along vegetating. Realize that your body cells react to all your sensations, just like a child.

If you never praise your child, but constantly rebuke and scold it, that it is good for nothing, it becomes listless and fearful. Finally, it itself believes that it is good for nothing. With this, your child develops complexes and cannot develop its talents.

Your cell children react in a similar way. If you lament continuously about your illnesses and troubles, if you talk to your neighbor about your troubles and illnesses and if you perform your daily work in a sullen, disgruntled, grumbling and listless manner, you will surely not encourage your cell children or activate the life force in them. On the contrary, you will rebuff the ether powers of the Spirit, which want to serve you lovingly. Your cell children, which listen to your sensations, thoughts and words, will answer you according to your behavior, either with health and activity or by becoming listless, weak and sick, because you constantly complain that they can never do anything right.

Consider, if you say: "I live," your cells will say the same. If you say: "I am weak, sick and tired," your cell state will say this, as well.

Remember: If you complain about your self-created causes, your cell children also sense this, and, over the course of time, behave accordingly, becoming tired and weak, because you constantly make them believe that they are incompetent.

*Finishing the healing meditation –
Subsequent thoughts and actions*

Before you rise from your healing meditation, first thank God, the Spirit in you. Do not immediately start working full strength.

Try to think and act in a harmonious and balanced way. Know that the Spirit is the fuel, the energy for your soul and the physical body. Thus, the soul is the motor and the physical body is the vehicle in which it is active. Try to start the motor of your life slowly. Do not demand a high performance right away. Let

God, the Spirit, be active through your soul and your physical body. When you become aware that the Spirit of God wants to feel, think and act through you, you will grant Him time and space for this.

Remember that all your base thoughts and motivations are registered not only by your cells, but also by your soul. With this continuous wrongdoing, you reduce the high ether powers, the Spirit, in you. If you then invoke these powers, it is not possible for them to support you fully right away. With your trusting cooperation, the awakening energies in you must first clear out the "rubbish," the negative vibrations, in your soul and in your body. This means, in turn, that the Spirit first has to absorb these unlawful vibration-structures, before He can bring your cells into action.

Do not forget that the Spirit carries out everything lovingly and in a lawful process. Therefore, be patient and practice patience if you have not yet mastered it, because patience is also a characteristic of God, which is present in all seven consciousness centers as ether power.

The correct use of medicines and medicinal herbs

As revealed, the ether power, the divine, flows in every life form.

If the Inner Physician cannot become fully effective yet, the human being should, nevertheless, not reach thoughtlessly for medicine right away, despite pain and illness. Recognize that often, too many medicines again reduce the developing and beneficial ether powers. As support for your health, O human being, reach first for the herbs of life and apply them in accordance with the spiritual law, which says: Let God, your Lord, be and work in the center of your life. Turn to God, your Father, with the acquired herbs, so that He may bless them and you can receive the thus increased healing power for the benefit of your body. Although the ether powers are constantly flowing in the herbs, as well as in all life forms, maintaining them, the healing powers can be increased many times over, if you ask God, Your Lord, for His blessing, that is, for strengthening the ether powers in the herbs.

If you have a toothache, rinse out your mouth with lukewarm horsetail tea. Moreover, fill a little linen bag with oat straw, horsetail and chamomile in equal amounts. Lay this bag, well warmed, on your cheek.

If the toothache does not go away and you have to take medicine, do not take the full dose right away, but only a half or a quarter of it.

Raise the herbs as well as the medicines to God, Your Lord, whose Spirit dwells in you, and ask for His blessing. What effect does the blessing have on the herbs and medicines? Especially the Spirit powers in the herbs come into higher vibration because everything consists of spirit. This means that the herbs receive even more Spirit power through the blessing. Everything that is brought into a higher vibration through the blessing power of God, which the child asks for trustingly, is even more effective.

Chemical medicines are permeated with only little Spirit power. Yet, if the child of God who entrusts himself completely to the Inner Physician, even though he does not yet fully stand under the all-permeating grace, asks for the blessing of the medicine, the Spirit power can fully unfold even in this medicine. A true, and strongly trusting devotion to the All-Highest, who dwells in the body and soul of every person, increases the inner effect of the medicine so that only a part of it is needed.

The harmful substances of the medicine can no longer affect the body cells much, since they now develop according to the rhythm of the Spirit, with the devotion to the All-One. Here, it has to be again stated that whether spirit or matter, everything is based on vibration. The Spirit power is the highest vibrating ether; matter is transformed down ether. Through a positive attitude and a corresponding way of life, the material vibration can be raised. This means that little by little, it adapts to the highest vibrating ether powers. In this way, these can become effective in the soul and person more quickly.

The life is in the herbs –
The ether power is
the best remedy

Before you take herbs, roots or other life forms from the forests or fields, you should first ask them for their gift, because, just as in you, the spiritual life flows in every life form.

With a sharp knife, cut these awakened life forms off at the root or the stalk. Treat them kindly and remember that they hold valuable ether powers.

The more you align with the ether power, the more it will be effective in the herbs and life forms.

Through your increased alignment with the ether powers, you will soon realize that the quantity of healing herbs you need decreases ever more, because then, the ether powers become more active in you, as well. By living a lawful life, you can continue to increase these holy powers in you.

The ether power is the best remedy. It makes all external aids, including medicinal herbs and plants, superfluous. Therefore, appeal again and again to the Inner Physician and Healer, to the holy ether powers that are flowing in you. They bear everything within themselves and they mix the inner powers in such a way that they are the best and most well-balanced medicine for you, because the One who dwells in you knows the exact dose you need in order to strengthen your soul and body and to keep your body healthy or help it become healthy.

The various effects of the sun's radiation

A person with weak nerves should never lie in the blazing sun when its radiation is very intense.

Every continent has different kinds of metals and materials that partially form, structure and influence the Earth's magnetic field. Every continent has its typical interaction with the sun. Especially at noontime, the magnetic field of a continent that is turned toward the sun has an increased interaction with the sun's corona that is comprised of many different kinds of vibrations. Through this interaction between continent and sun, a specific frequency in the sun's corona is addressed, which then increases its activity and releases the corresponding forces for this continent.

During this time rich in eruptions, the corresponding frequency in the sun's corona expels very many sun particles that are charged with high energy. These reach the Earth and enter the life forms, either via direct radiation or via the magnetic currents. They penetrate the Earth, human beings and also animals, if they are exposed to the blazing sun around noontime, causing a state of increased activity in human beings and animals that can lead to strong aggressions.

This increased heat energy can also disturb the magnetic field of the body, which may trigger various indispositions and illnesses, such as headache, circulatory disorders, heart failure, blood stasis and nervous tension. The stomach, spleen and pancreas, as well as all other glands and hormones can develop disorders through the disharmonious magnetic field of the body. Likewise, wrong reactions can be the result of this high magnetic tension.

Increased solar radiation can also lead to facial erysipelas and shingles, which are basically a nervous disorder. They can also be caused, among other things, by food that is exposed to the sun at noon, especially during the summer months, or which was under the strong influence of magnetic currents by being stored at too high a temperature. Fruits, vegetables, grains and all foods that are stored in warm rooms or in the sun are enriched with energy particles that can contribute to the development of illnesses.

Both of the aforementioned illnesses can also develop as the result of the increased activity of the thyroid gland and hormones or through overstrained nerves, which are often the result of a too strong radiation of sun particles in the body. An increased solar radiation and absorption of these highly enriched energetic sun particles can also lead to disorders of the thyroid gland and an increased activation of hormones. The result is increased sensuality, which is clearly discernible in very hot countries. Unknowing souls of the deceased (astral souls) with a similar temperament, then go to these vibrations of increased sensuality, which can influence people and drive them to this vice even more. Especially during the summer months, a large part of the sun particles is deflected by the cloud layers toward countries with a lot of sun. The remaining sun particles are weakened by the cloud layers and penetrate the Earth, people, animals and all material life forms only to a lesser degree.

Hunting and killing of wild game at noontime, especially during the summer months, is harmful, not only for the hunter, but also for those who eat the prey, regardless of how long it was boiled, roasted or fried. The meat that is charged with disharmonious, active sun particles is harmful, above all, for the nervous system, particularly the autonomic nervous system. This injury to the nervous system can result in various illnesses, among other things. Skin cancer, leukemia and cancer of the organs may be caused by disharmonious sun particles. The same can happen if a person exposes himself to the blazing sun at noon for an extended period of time.

Fruits or vegetables harvested during these energy-laden noon hours are also strongly charged with these disharmonious forces and are therefore harmful to human beings and animals.

Frozen food that is thawed in the sun is interwoven by the energy of the sun particles. Especially on hot days during the summer months they are in disorder and disharmony. They induce illnesses in the nerves and in those organs strongly influenced by the nerves.

During intense sun radiation a person should not wear clothes made of synthetic fibers. The sun's rays that come in contact with this fabric cause an accumulation of heat that has a harmful effect on the highly sensitive nervous system.

However, cotton fibers neutralize and balance the tension, among other things, because cotton is in the range of vibration of the sun's energy. This means that the solar particles are in harmony with cotton fibers as well as wool fibers.

Working with synthetic materials under solar radiation or in overheated rooms also has a similarly disturbing effect on the person. Manifold illnesses can be the result, since every body vibrates at a different rate and, therefore, has its own specific magnetic field, depending on the person's way of life.

However, the sun particles that fall on the Earth, on human beings and animals at sunrise are refreshing for the dwelling planet and its inhabitants. These particles, which penetrate the Earth and its life in the morning, bear the harmonizing and upbuilding power of the sun. A person who knows how to absorb these energetic particles receives life-strengthening and beneficial energetic powers.

When a continent turns away from the sun, thus, already at the time of sunset, an increased number of moon particles strike the Earth that lend people a restful sleep, particularly before midnight. The person who goes to sleep after midnight already receives sun particles that are highly charged with energy. These stimulate the activity of the nerves, thus causing a restless sleep, filled with dreams.

The moon particles that are absorbed by the sleeping person before midnight calm the soul and body. If a person is walking the path of purification of the soul, these processes during sleep facilitate the separation of the soul from the body as well as the soul's ascent into soul realms filled with higher energy, thus bringing about a quicker purification of the soul. At the same time, the magnetic currents that flow more calmly before midnight have a calming effect on the human body and thus, a healing effect on the nerves. After midnight, however, the magnetic currents of the Earth increase their activity again and have a negative influence on the person who goes to bed very late.

About the thyroid gland and its treatment

The thyroid gland is an organ that should be treated very cautiously. It can change the entire balance of the body, as well the body itself. Very often, your moods also depend on the activity of the thyroid gland. The treatment of this gland with wrong medication can have a harmful effect on hormones and glands. Therefore, I advise you to be especially cautious with this organ. If this gland is treated incorrectly during young years, this can have corresponding effects in old age.

The cells and hormones can be impaired by improper treatment of the thyroid gland, particularly in women whose body functions are changing. An unlawful way of life can also cause such disorders, which then provoke many different ailments in elderly people, for instance, emaciation or corpulence.

The thyroid gland reacts to drinks that are too hot as well as too cold. It signals its well-being or malaise to the whole cell structure and above all, to the hormones and glands, which thereby slowly grow weak and can no longer carry out their proper function.

The same is true if a person drinks large quantities of alcohol or eats fatty, very spicy, and above all, very salty food. If a lot of animal food is eaten and not chewed properly, disorders in a person's general condition can be caused by the thyroid gland. All these factors contribute to a slackening of the cell structure and impairment in the activity of the glands and hormones. These deficiencies often do not become apparent until midlife, in women as well as men. However, they occur more often in women, since the activity of the reproductive organs decreases.

Therefore, O human being, eat moderately and chew your food well; do not season it too strongly, especially not with hot spices. Drink moderately, if possible no alcohol, but good fruit juices. Fruit juices in particular build up the cells and are also refreshing for your glands and hormones. Drink cherry and apricot juice. They have a high ether content, if they were treated properly. Good apple juice also contributes to the elimination of toxins and promotes the activity of cells, glands and hormones in the right measure.

If a person lives a life according to the laws of God, all the organs of the body will function properly. But often, a person realizes this only when he has reached an advanced age, in which glandular and hormonal functions decrease.

I will now name several kinds of teas that bring about the proper activity of the thyroid gland. However, I would like to add that these teas have different effects on individual people.

For a hypothyroid condition: bedstraw, vervain, lesser centaury, hemp nettle, comfrey, silverweed, lovage, marshmallow, five-leaf grass.

Take from these teas 3 or 4 cups of each, and mix them in equal portions. Drink approximately 2 cups a day, lukewarm and in sips. Change the tea after about 4-6 weeks. If possible, drink without sugar. If you would like to sweeten it, use wild honey or fruit sugar sparingly.

For a hyperthyroid condition: silverweed, hops, celandine, ribwort plantain, coltsfoot, oxlip, wild chicory, barberry, motherwort, gentian. Blend only up to four kinds and proceed as revealed above.

In many cases, the time at which they are harvested is very important, as well as the conditions under which they are dried. The human being seldom makes the effort to gather the herbs for his own use. He usually goes to herbalists and has to take what is offered. However, if a person is devoted to God, and if his soul was prepared through a corresponding way of life so that the inner source of the spirit flows in him to a higher degree, then by requesting the blessing of the herbs, much that vibrates negatively is lessened and the positive life force in the herbs increased.

Our Lord said: "Do this in memory of Me!" However, a person should not only pray for the blessing of his bread, but of everything that God has let grow and flourish through His light, including medicinal plants.

The effectiveness of the blessing power in the herbs and also in the food truly brings about a transformation in them. Without a person seeing it, low, unlawful vibrations become powerless, and high vibrations receive an even higher vibrating power. In this way, the ingredients of the food and medicinal plants have an even more intense effect on the organs and cells of the body.

*Get to know the anatomy
of your soul body and activate
the consciousness centers*

When a person knows about the activity of the Spirit in the various consciousness centers, he can receive spiritual energy directly from them and far more quickly than if he turns to the omnipresent ether streams only in a general way. Therefore, as already revealed, a person should be experienced with the anatomy of his body as well as that of his soul. If you know the anatomical make-up of your body, you can often very quickly analyze which organ causes you pain, and can take direct countermeasures.

If you have heart trouble, for instance, you should know which of the seven consciousness centers is wrongly polarized, so that you can activate it and pray that the healing ether powers for your heart come from there. Thus, a human being should also know the anatomy of his soul body so that he knows which spiritual center is affecting the respective organs, if he has a sore throat, toothache, or pain in the nose or ears, etc.

God is Spirit! The seven consciousness centers correspond to the natures and attributes of God. In each center in which they are flowing, the ether powers have a different vibration and their frequencies are tuned to the individual organs of the body.

If you, O human being, want to illuminate a large room, you will also use several sources of light that differ in intensity. In one part, a small light is sufficient; in another part you need a stronger light. It depends on what kind of activity you want to carry out in the various parts of the room.

The ether powers of the Spirit flow in the same diversity. Each of the wheels of consciousness, that is, each nature or attribute of God, has its specific rate of vibration, which is also expressed in its light intensity.

Provided you know your soul body and have learned to invoke your consciousness centers, help can be bestowed on you significantly faster, because you immediately recognize which nature or attribute of God you have violated.

For instance, if a person has a weak heart, he assuredly acted against the fourth consciousness center in this life or in one of his previous lives. This energy field, the center of divine Earnestness, is also where the Redeemer-Spark of Christ is active. Although the effects of the individual offenses may vary – since the streams of divine Earnestness also flow in the other consciousness centers, not as primary, but as secondary energy – the offenses mostly make themselves felt with a polarity reversal of the respective primary center. A knowing person, who is experienced with the anatomy of his soul body, will therefore vivify this primary center, but also think about how he can dissolve this reversal of polarity, or shadowing, in his soul. He will not only address the ether powers in the affected energy field, but also purify the ether channels of the soul and those of the body with a corresponding life, by analyzing his way of life and by changing his human habits.

If the human being has violated the sixth consciousness center, the energy field of Love, he will have eye, nasal or cerebral ailments, for example, when the karma flows out.

If he has mainly violated the streams of the fifth consciousness center, illnesses in the area of the tonsils, thyroid gland, larynx, throat, or perhaps of the lungs, and so forth, will occur.

It is often the case that a person has violated several divine basic powers. The result is that several organs become ill and mental depression can occur. The root cause, however, is the shadowing of the soul, which results in the weakening of the consciousness center's activity and the person's organs being supplied with only very little ether powers.

A very strenuous life causes the energy that a person gains through nutrition or medication to be used up very quickly through an unlawful way of thinking and speaking. Since the consciousness centers are inactive because of the dense shadowing and are therefore largely impenetrable to the Spirit powers, the ether powers cannot stimulate and strengthen to offset this. As a result of this and like processes, the organs of the body become weak all the more quickly and fall ill much easier.

Therefore, when a person knows about these lawful processes and endeavors to change his way of life by aligning with the divine laws, when he activates the corresponding consciousness centers lawfully and is also able to direct the ether powers by the power of thought, he is far ahead of all other people who pray. But all this should be done in the name, and according to the will, of the Lord. However, may the person program himself and direct the holy ether powers only after he has spoken some heartfelt words of surrender to God, our Lord.

A prayer request becomes effective, however, only when a person surrenders his self-will to God, his Lord, and is willing to let the divine will in him become effective. This is why the one seeking help should always finish his prayer request with the addition: "But, Lord, may Your will be done, because You alone know what is good and helpful for my soul and my body."

*Further instructions for
activating the fifth consciousness center –
Larynx, vocal cords, breathing*

The one who has problems with his larynx should also address the fifth consciousness center. Most of all, he should program his cells, which means, as I already explained, to align them with the ether powers so that they open their cell mouths and willingly receive the divine power flowing from the fifth energy center.

You can also train the vocal cords. Place the sounds of God on them by saying, for instance: "God," or "Amen, life, Spirit and power." Or: "oh – oh, ah – ah – ah," or "la" or "Father, Order, Will, Grace, Love." Since the interaction of the divine life is in all cells, every cell reacts to the sensations and thoughts of the person. This is why you can consciously address all cells. They will react. Begin by speaking to your vocal cords as follows:

I, your body, ask you, vocal cords, to joyfully accept my words that I place on you. Let the words vibrate and open yourselves to the powers of the Spirit.

Now, O human being, first place the word "God" on your vocal cords. In the larynx say: "God, God, God," and link at the same time with the fifth consciousness center, which is in the neck area. Let the high vibration of the word "God" penetrate to your fifth energy field and let it likewise vibrate in your head. Ask the ether Spirit, which is active in the fifth consciousness center, to vivify your vocal cords. Do not allow any thoughts to enter you. Remain in this salutary and vitalizing, flowing wellspring of the Spirit.

Place a further word on your vocal cords, for instance, "Father," and with this highly vibrating word again address the fifth power field.

Practice this exercise several times a day.

May it become a habit to place all words on the vocal cords, and, from the larynx, speak them into your head. Then you will soon feel that your breathing is also changing and becoming perfect.

As a support for your vocal cords, you can gargle with horsetail and sage tea. A tea made of marshmallow and lovage is also advisable.

If you do all this in a deep and soulful belief in God, in Christ, your Inner Physician and Healer, you will assuredly be successful. Of course, persistence and a life of devotion and surrender to God, our Lord, are also a part of this.

When a person strives for a well-regulated breathing, he often uses many techniques that are more hindrance than benefit for him to truly speak and breathe. Remember, O human being, that the Spirit, which dwells and wants to become effective in you, can do anything. He can also give you the correct way of breathing. His perfect, spiritual respiration dissolves the tensions in you. In this way, the Spirit can then respirate and breathe through your entire body, that is, through each and every cell thoroughly.

Therefore, O human being, first of all, train a correct manner of speaking. Place your words on the vocal cords; let them vibrate there and then let them vibrate in your whole head. The result will be a strong breathing! Make it a habit to sit and to walk in an upright manner. Your steps should be measured and harmonious. Your eyes should not be directed only at the ground, but into the distance so that you can perceive the fullness of infinity. Refine your sensations and thoughts. Then your breathing will be perfect, solely by the power of the Lord, without learning any special breathing technique.

Provided you have now learned to address all seven consciousness centers and you lead a lawful life in your feeling, thinking, speaking and acting, paying attention to the right eating habits and chewing and drinking correctly, you will soon notice that the Spirit of God not only respirates you, but breathes throughout all your organs and cells. The one who continues to live by these principles will soon recognize that improper breathing techniques lead to tensions elsewhere, for it is the breath of the Spirit, that is, the conscious breathing of the Spirit in you, which really sets you free.

As soon as the person doubts the powers of the Inner Physician and Healer and talks with others about his illnesses, suffering or blows of fate, instead of speaking with Christ in God, our Lord, he can be sure that his illness will not go away. Doubting in the All-power of God and a lot of talk about illnesses and worries do not bring the desired blessing to a person. Whatever wants to flow out and dissolve is held back in the physical body or in the soul through this wrong way of feeling, thinking and acting.

The Spirit of God in you is always ready to serve you. The greatest hindrance can be you, O human being! An example: When the sun shines into the rooms of your home, it illuminates every dark corner of your room. But if you close the shutters, your room becomes dark and cool. Oh recognize that it is similar in you. If your disposition is bright and filled with trust in the divine help, if you do not fear possible illnesses and blows of fate and do not talk about them, either, the light of God will penetrate your soul as well as your body to a higher degree. It will gradually illuminate and remove all still hidden illnesses and blows of fate that are building up.

The Spirit is eternally vivifying energy. The person has to open himself to these powers of God and may not close the shutters, that is, cover the cells and soul particles with counteractive vibrations through an unlawful way of thinking, speaking and acting, thus denying to the light of the Spirit the possibility to penetrate, soothe and heal. The awakened person who lives and thinks in the Spirit of God can thus address every center and call up the healing, helpful ether powers directly – provided he aspires to a consistent life in God.

As already revealed, the tonsils, thyroid gland, larynx, throat, teeth and, in part, the lungs, can be supplied with ether powers via the fifth consciousness center, which is located in the neck region. The ether powers also flow into the arms and hands via this power field.

About the fourth center of consciousness

In the fourth consciousness center, the energy field of divine Earnestness, the Christ-Redeemer-light is active. This spiritual power field, located in the back region between the shoulder blades and near the heart, is a very strongly rotating and pulsating center that is also the connection between the sixth consciousness center, which is located between the eyes, and the first three consciousness powers, which are active below this Christ-center. This fourth consciousness center transports the holy ether powers from the collective basin in the region of the coccyx, upward to the sixth power field, the center of Love, which guides the holy powers to the seventh wheel of consciousness. From there, they finally again reach the core of being of God in the innermost part of the soul. Thus the spiritual-physical circulation of energy of divine ether is completed.

The spiritual body, which is called soul as long as it is burdened, has a completely balanced circulation of energy. Only once this circulation of the cosmic powers in the soul absolutely moves in the rhythm of the divine law and these cosmic streams flow according to the seven times seven cosmic life forces, will the soul have again become a pure spirit being and one with the Infinite.

The following organs are supplied with ether powers via the fourth consciousness center: heart, lungs, spinal cord and ribs. I would like to point out that the ether powers also vivify the glands, hormones, all cells, as well as the layers of skin and the bones of the human body, via every center and in accordance with the person's devotion to God. The eternally flowing Spirit endeavors to fully permeate the whole human being and to control matter. Only when the Spirit can radiate through matter, the physical body, to a great extent, because the God-seeker devotes himself to the Infinite, will the body maintain its elasticity and health despite an advanced age.

The person can address the heart via the fourth power field and pray, for instance, with such words as the following:

Father, I am Your child. You are the Absoluteness in me. You are the perfect Spirit who has created only perfection. Our human ailments, no matter what they might be, occurred and still occur only because we are far from God, since we have turned away from the eternally giving, maintaining and perfect law of life. This is why my heart is not in order and my blood circulation is subject to great fluctuations. O Spirit, You, who are my Father, pour Your holy and healing powers into my weak and sick heart by way of the fourth consciousness center. I ask You to increase Your ether power, so that I become healthy, provided it is Your will.

If, in addition, you now address your heart, that is, the cells of your heart, the children of your body, you, yourself, can also be very helpful.

Through their wrong way of feeling, thinking, speaking and acting, people have often directed the attention of the components of their bodies totally to without, so that the cell children are not at all accustomed to listening to the high ether powers in their innermost being and to entirely opening themselves to these powers. By constantly complaining about pain and the like, people have not conveyed encouraging thought-powers to their cell children. Quite the contrary, due to people's wrong way of thinking and acting, the cells became tired and react to hardly anything but food or medication.

However, the one who asks the Inner Physician and Healer for advice and help should also have encouraging thoughts and words for his sick body, which will then benefit his cell children. As a result, they will gradually align with the Inner Physician and Healer, who soothes and heals via the seven basic centers.

Therefore, if it is recommended to align with God, your Father in Christ, your Inner Physician and Healer, this means that you should change in your feelings, thoughts, words and also in your actions, so that your cell children turn more and more to the ether powers, to the Inner Physician and Healer, instead of practicing their previous outwardly oriented habits.

*Further instructions for activating
the fourth center of consciousness –
Heart and circulatory problems*

Try to also lead a healthy life. Attach great importance to upbuilding, highly vibrating food.

For heart disease and a poor circulation of the blood, prepare yourself a meal made of barley or oats, or of rye and rice. Also eat wholegrain bread – the best would be bread of coarsely ground grain, but take care that it is not too old or already moldy. You should not eat food that has mold on it, because fungi and ferments will develop that are not good for your heart, in particular, but also your lungs. These pathogens, which appear in a variety of ways, are transported into the whole body via the blood, which can lead to illnesses in several areas of your body.

Especially people with heart disease, circulatory problems and diseases of the lungs should attach importance to foods low in calories and fats.

A God-seeker who entrusts himself to the Inner Physician and Healer should lead a healthy life, that is, he should nourish himself with only those things nature willingly gives him – mainly fruit and grain, for instance.

The person who has turned to God should never overeat. This means, he should not indulge in gluttony or feasting, but should eat moderately and thank God, our Lord, for His gifts of grace, because everything that human beings receive from the hands of the Lord is grace.

For the weakness of the heart muscle or a general cardiac insufficiency, the following teas can be recommended: lovage, motherwort, lesser centaury, silverweed, bedstraw, horsetail and violets. Choose four kinds, blend them and drink approximately two cups of tea per day. Drink them lukewarm, without sugar, for 4-6 weeks.

I must point out again and again that the Spirit gives only general directions. If the desired results do not come, the person should remember that this may have to do with the nature of his soul burden or with his present way of life that does not comply with the laws of God. The Spirit does not interfere with the existing worldly law by giving these instructions. The Spirit merely gives advice from the great active law of God, which permeates all things. This law of God has given humankind the maintaining principle of life – the healing and nourishing powers of the nature kingdom.

To strengthen a weak heart, the heart area can be rubbed with rubbing alcohol containing dwarf mountain pine. Afterwards, the one who seeks healing should wear warm clothes; especially the heart, the entire chest area, should be kept warm. With cardiac and circulatory problems, it is very important that feet and head are kept warm because a warm head and warm feet eliminate many illnesses.

*There is no illness in the
domain of the Spirit – Fear and worries
open the door wide for illness*

The power of the Holy Spirit is in every cell. This means that in every cell of the entire organism there are spiritual powers. These powers of the Spirit have two basic forces, the positive and negative poles, as human beings know from the polarity of the Earth. If these two basic forces are in harmony, they are in constant harmonious interaction. Through the interaction of these poles, energy and life develop.

There are also two spiritual poles in every cell of the body, also called positive and negative. The Spirit also calls them the two basic powers of eternal life. The divine ether – which is first forwarded via the core of being in the soul to the seven consciousness centers, and from there via the ether tree to the body cells – touches these two basic powers in the cells. This causes the cell membranes to vibrate. The more Spirit powers flow into the body cells, the more intensely the cell membranes vibrate and the more dynamic the person's body is. This dynamism of the Spirit powers brings about harmony in the entire cell structure, in the nerves and in all organs. These dynamic powers of God keep the physical body healthy.

If these healing powers can flow unhindered into body and soul from God, from the core of being of the soul, they do not allow pathogens to penetrate the body, or they transport them quickly out of the body. Wherever the Spirit rules unimpeded, illnesses can neither exist nor develop. The cell children react to the divine ether powers and do not allow themselves to be influenced by the low vibrations of pathogens, unless the person opens the way for these low frequencies with his negative inclinations and base feelings and actions. And so, O human being, your noble and pure sensations, thoughts, words and deeds are the doorkeepers.

You, yourself, O child of God, are the policeman for your cell state, that is, the doorkeeper of your life. A good policeman knows about the laws of the Spirit and also applies them accordingly. An unknowing person, who is merely called policeman or doorkeeper by name, will not apply the laws of God, and will therefore open the way for base vibrations, the viruses, bacteria, and many other unknown pathogens. In addition, a person animates these base vibrations by talking about his illnesses and being afraid of any and all negativity. These pathogens may be stimulated into activity and the vibration of the cell structure may be diminished just through lengthy, negative talking and acting. Besides, fear and worries reduce the dynamic energy in the cells, which means that the cells, in turn, become fearful and anxious and weaken more and more.

Therefore, if the cell structure becomes weakened by unlawful thoughts and actions, the penetrating pathogens are hereby encouraged, because fear and worries attract negative powers. Therefore, O human being, speak to your cells as to children. Encourage them and explain to them what high powers dwell in them, which are just waiting to unfold and become active.

Instructions for illnesses of the lungs –
Rules for a short and an extended meditation

If you, O human being, feel an illness in your lungs, for example, or suffer other complaints, keep up your courage and do not think the worst. Fearful thoughts do not bring joy to the cells of your lungs and do not orient them to the active ether powers. Your person and also your cell children become discouraged by this. You, and your cells as well, open up to illnesses or blows of fate, which do not necessarily press for manifestation as karma. On the contrary: If there was no blow of fate and no illness indicated in your book of life, in the karmic book of your soul, you have evoked this illness or misfortune merely by your wrong way of thinking and wrong conduct in this earthly existence. Actions, that is, negative ways of thinking and acting, cause reactions. They attract low vibrations that then build up in you. For instance: If you have sent angry, base thoughts to your fellowman, he will be touched by these thoughts, insofar as he is on the frequency of your vibrations.

Therefore, live in harmony with yourself and your neighbor, and then you will also live in harmony with your whole body, with all the organs, cells, glands and hormones. The harmonization of your whole being will then lead you to unity, into absolute harmony with the Infinite, who dwells in you.

For this reason, talk to your lungs, as you talk to all organs:

You, great breathing organ, that have a place near the heart, the great power station in the human being, be aware of your high task in my body. In every lung vesicle, in every cell, vibrates the high power of the Spirit. This energy is our mutual source, from which we drink and refresh ourselves.

Now, you two lungs, open yourselves for the powers of the holy ether. They are our life. We may now drink of these powers of the Spirit. They give us strength and power.

O human being, devote yourself to a short meditation several times a day!

You have the possibility to do this everywhere, no matter where you may be:

At your place of work, in your home, or even while you are shopping. For a short time, you can walk slowly, for instance, along a side street. Immerse yourself in the power of God. Ask God for His life-breath, for your lungs, for example. Ask God, your Father, to breathe consciously through you. During this short time, around five minutes, forget your surroundings and all that you still have to get. Let "It" breathe in you. Think lovingly of your sick organ, the lungs, and be aware that God, the Lord, strengthens them. Via your sensations, you can establish a divine connection with the fourth consciousness center, the center of Earnestness, also called the Christ-center. From there, you can ask for the direct power and healing streams.

Since everything is based on vibration, you will be able to bring the fourth consciousness center into raised activity through *one* God-filled thought. Spiritual energy will then flow directly into your sick organ from this potential of powers.

As already revealed, the Christ-center fulfills a high function in your body. Via these pulsating Christ-powers, the person and his soul find the absolute redemption and liberation, including liberation from illness and sorrows, because this center provides all other spiritual-physical energy fields with life forces, according to your way of life, that is, according to your feelings, thoughts, words and actions. You can apply the technique of invocation and immersion for every organ, and also for your overtaxed nerves!

In case you have the peace for a longer meditation, assume the meditation position. Turn your face to the east and address your lungs, as I have already revealed, bringing them into connection with the fourth consciousness center. If it is possible to meditate in the open air during the summer months, or even in a fir forest or a garden under spruce or pine trees, you will receive their odic forces in addition. Nature and all forms of creation of the Spirit give willingly and in great abundance to the most beautiful child of creation, the child of the divine Father, provided the person recognizes himself as part of the great totality and is in harmony and at peace with all divine life forms.

In case you have weak lungs and the ether powers have not yet become so effective in you that they can take remedial action, it is advisable that twice a week you cover yourself with earth during the mid-morning hours, when the earth has been warmed by the sun's radiation, and then remain so for ten minutes. Afterward, you should take a bath containing the fresh shoots of pines and fir trees. Take a third bath once a week with the shoots, but without covering yourself with earth. The same treatment is valid for tuberculosis of the bones.

You can also use young fir shoots to inhale. Bring the shoots to a brief boil and then inhale the rising vapors.

Dear brothers and sisters, please do not carelessly break off the shoots from the tree, the work of our Creator! Cut them off lovingly with a sharp knife. In every life form is the power of the Spirit. Ask the Spirit in the fir tree for a part of the shoots. Then cut off a few shoots at an angle. Please do not take off all the shoots from the branches because the tree also wants to adorn itself every year with a new garment, which lets it become larger and stronger. Take shoots from several trees and only a very few from each tree. Half a handful is sufficient for 2-3 inhalations! Take only very young shoots for inhalation, and do not inhale more than 2-3 times a week. For a bath, you can mix the shoots used for inhalation with fir extracts, which you can buy at specialty stores.

If you are prone to bronchitis and have weak lungs, you should lie in the shade in fresh, not yet quite dry, hay at midday for approximately 15 minutes, 3-4 times a week.

In order to cure illnesses of the lungs or to strengthen the lungs, the Spirit recommends that in winter you rub the body in the region of the lungs with snow at midday. Subsequently dry off the body and envelop it in warm clothes. Angora woolen underwear is best. Then remain in a warm room so that the body can develop strong heat through the angora underwear. You can use the same treatment when suffering from bronchitis.

The strong healing powers of the sun and the moon are effective in the snow. It is the sun and moon particles that fall to the Earth.

This is why the application of snow, as revealed above, is best done at noon, after the sun has transmitted its warming rays to the snow.

It is crucial that a person consciously follow all these instructions given here, believing in the One who dwells in his innermost being, in God, our Father, whose children we all are.

I repeat: This spiritual healing method can be applied by every human child. Since the spirit powers flow differently in every human being, however, the healing effects will not be the same in every case. One seeker for healing is more devoted to God, the other less. With one person, a soul burden must first flow out; with another, it may be a weak faith.

As far as herbal teas are concerned, for which the Spirit merely makes suggestions, the human being should know: These gifts of God are gifts of grace. Only the one who recognizes them as such will feel their effect. You should not think that they must be salutary and effective just because the Spirit points them out. This depends exclusively on the devotion to God by the one seeking healing and on the nature of the soul's burden.

Since every soul body and every physical body is burdened differently and therefore, reacts differently, these healing revelations do not exclude the consultation of a doctor.

Now I will mention several kinds of tea that strengthen the lungs and the bronchia: Lungwort, white hawthorn, oat straw, mistletoe, dandelion, thistle and ribwort plantain. Choose up to five kinds of herbs; blend and drink two cups during the day, lukewarm. This is an additional remedy for people with weak lungs.

Tea made of onions, sweetened with wild honey and drunk quite warm, is a good tonic for the heart, and also loosens the mucus.

Composure – An upright posture – Physical exercises

The spinal cord and your ribs are also irradiated by the healing ether powers of God.

Strive to walk upright, regardless of whether your body is young or has grown old. Make it your habit to assume a meditative posture when walking. Walk upright!

Strive to practice permanent self-control. Practice that you do not fall into a hectic pace or let anyone rush you. The balance of your soul and of your physical body will give you composure in all things and, at the same time, allow for purposeful activity. Arrange your life and your daily routine in such a way that you can do everything in harmony. Know that your work is not done more quickly if you do it in a hectic and disharmonious way. On the contrary, you will work without a goal and aimlessly. In this way, many things in your daily plan will not be accomplished. Every bit of restlessness that you send out also disturbs the harmony of your body, and hinders the increased flow of the salutary ether powers.

If your body structure is feeble and if most of your work is done while sitting, do not forget to do simple physical exercises daily, for instance in the morning, at noon and in the evening. Your body will be grateful to you, especially in later years. Simple harmonious exercises loosen your whole body structure. Your organs will relax, which, in turn, has the effect that you can breathe more easily and buoyantly, and in addition, the ether powers can contribute their part. The effects can be enhanced if you do your exercises to very harmonious music. That gives you a double effect. If you are devoted to God, your Lord, and if you commend yourself to Him in prayer every morning, your cell children will rejoice over the conscious, harmonious physical exercises done to melodic music. They will turn to the ether powers more intensely and open themselves to them.

A person should do everything consciously, that is, aware of the presence of God.

If a person devotes himself to God, his Father, each day and also proves to be a child of God in his daily life, by respecting his neighbor and acknowledging him as his brother, he will soon feel the balm of life; that is, the holy and healing ether powers will flow through him more intensely, nourishing, vivifying, healing and serving him.

The motto of your life should be: Lord, speak and act through me.

The Spirit wants to permeate matter, to act and predominate in human beings. Oh, let this be done, so that you, O human being, may attain bliss while still in the earthly garment.

*The second and third
consciousness centers*

The third consciousness center is in the lumbar region. It encompasses the spinal column with the spinal cord and the abdominal area with stomach, small intestines, liver, spleen and pancreas.

The eternally flowing Spirit is active in all the cells, organs, hormones and glands, in the bones, in the bone marrow, in the whole organism. His divine powers permeate everything in the same measure as the person turns to these ether powers. Thus, they flow differently in every body, as already revealed, in one person more strongly, in another less so. The one person has a mature, balanced soul, through which the holy ether powers flow more intensely and thus, can become effective in the body quickly. The soul of another is more shadowed and therefore clouded, so the ether powers cannot become active so quickly.

In every human being, and in every soul, divine grace, divine mercy and love are active.

With a constant devotion to the Godhead, the person who practices patience in his life and devotes himself to the healing powers of the Christ of God more each day, brings about an increased flow of God's grace. This grace creates more and more space in the person for the healing and life powers and is ready to reduce much negativity in him.

Therefore, may each person strive to lead a life in God's will, so that he can give the Spirit of God the possibility to unfold in him more and more.

The spiritual healing method is mainly based on these holy, divine ether powers, that is, on the development and guidance of the powers of the Holy Spirit, and less on the natural cure methods that are mentioned only briefly in this book. It is primarily the opening up of the spiritual life forces, the ether, which can achieve anything, provided it can flow in an unrestricted way. The Spirit of God in the human being is the best physician, healer, counselor, leader, guide and, above all, the loving Father of His devoted children.

From a spiritual-divine point of view, the third consciousness center is called the center of Wisdom. Without this spiritual energy field, the human bone structure and muscular system would not be fully movable. The divine principle of Wisdom, this holy ether stream, brings about a person's upright and graceful way of walking. The divine Wisdom is likewise the deed. This can be recognized when we think of the active organs, like the stomach, intestines and so forth, provided with the holy ether powers via this consciousness center.

This consciousness center is also the origin of the human being's creativity; it touches a person's spirit. If this spirit is aligned with God and if the person asks for God's guidance and instruction, the streams of divine Wisdom, in particular, will unfold. They flow not only in the third consciousness center, but also, as a part of the sevenfold ether stream, in all other consciousness centers. In the Spirit, there is no separation of power. Everything is contained in the smallest, most insignificant particle, as well as in the great totality. Therefore, according to the spiritual laws, it is said: Everything is contained in all things! The power of Wisdom is stabilizing and strengthening. Someone who suffers from bone diseases or physical deformities has surely violated this strengthening, stabilizing spiritual law of the deed.

If the person suffers from the illnesses listed above, or if he has problems with his spinal column or spinal cord, etc., in his sensations, he should – provided he wants to attain healing via the ether powers – link these parts of the body or organs with the third consciousness center and should also become aware of the guilt of his soul. O human being, think over your life and recognize which powers of the law that are expressed in the consciousness centers, you have sinned against, and henceforth do this no more.

The spiritual treatment of the spinal column

Try, as much as this is possible for you, to walk upright. Keep your head erect. And have an upright sitting posture.

Talk to your vertebrae. Encourage them, because God, the life, is also in them. O human being, do not complain, because you alone are to blame, due to your own negative way of thinking and acting toward God, your Father, who is also the strength in your vertebrae. You can address each of the vertebrae. While doing this, try to touch it with the fingers of your right hand, as far as possible. Mentally link your spinal column with the divine powers in the third consciousness center, and ask this source of ether for relief or healing. Be aware that the divine Spirit is energy and, in accordance with the will of God and your sincere prayer thoughts, you can free up the reversed polarity of the spiritual channels leading to your spinal column. These holy powers can then flow more intensely into your organs or, as in this case, into your spinal column.

Every athlete should especially turn his attention to this third consciousness center of Wisdom, which is, at the same time, the energy field of the deed. It is primarily via this center that the muscular system is supplied with spirit powers. Also, the veins, tendons and nerves receive the ether powers via this third energy field.

Scientists and doctors, as well, should activate this third consciousness center in order to enhance their intuitive abilities, for it has a very strong effect on the solar plexus and, thus, on a person's disposition and feelings. The more active this third consciousness center is, the more sensitive and creative the person will be.

Every genuine Christ-healer receives the Christ-power from the fourth consciousness center. However, above all, a raised activity of the third consciousness center is necessary, as well as an increased effectiveness of the first and second energy fields, so that this healing power can flow more intensely to the one seeking healing via the fourth center. If the first three consciousness centers are largely active, great healing powers already flow in the healer. I repeat: The more strongly Order, Will and Wisdom are in action, the more Spirit powers, that is, healing powers, flow, also from the fourth center, which is also called the Christ-center. I do not, however, want to reveal the healing process in its totality here. These explanations are merely meant to give you an idea of it.

The more the first three consciousness centers are vivified and radiating, the more the sixth power field also rotates in the body. This consciousness center of Love is, as revealed, a switching point for guiding the ether powers to the other consciousness centers. It forms the direct access to the gate of Mercy, the seventh consciousness center, which receives the ether powers from the core of being of the soul. In this core of being, Love and Mercy fashion, beside the principle of Patience, the main streams of the divine ether power.

You, O human being, can address your spinal column lastingly with the following words:

You are the trunk of my body. You receive everything you need from the third center of consciousness. Drink from these powers and straighten yourself with these powers. I, your person, will assist you, by putting my life in order, in thought, as well as in words and deeds, helping you, the trunk of my body, to receive further upbuilding powers.

Daily, light physical exercises are strongly advised. Let your arms and legs circle; move your torso;

do several knee bends; strengthen your body and make it your habit to keep an upright, harmonious posture.

You can address your spinal cord in a similar manner as you did your vertebrae, and entrust it to the third consciousness center for an intensified provision of energy.

*Your digestive organ,
the stomach, also obeys the
third consciousness center*

Both your heart and your stomach have important functions in your body. Do not overtax your heart, or your stomach, either. Only when the human being has recognized that his oral cavity with its teeth is the pre-stomach, will his digestive organ, the stomach, be able to serve his body properly.

Chew your food slowly and supply it well with saliva. This will enrich the energy in your body, so that you can get along with a smaller quantity of food. Chewing sets free energy that will be led directly to the body. However, this holds true only when you chew consciously, that is, when you are silent during your meals and rest consciously in the divine presence.

Remember that the stomach has no teeth. It processes the food only with its muscles and gastric juices. Conscious and slow chewing brings about harmony not only in your stomach, but also in other organs that are linked to it, as well as in your heart and blood circulation.

The bigger the pieces that you hastily put into your mouth and chew only briefly and quickly, the more the stomach, the liver, the spleen, the small and the large intestines come into turmoil. The stomach, which senses the arrival of a large quantity of food chewed more or less hastily, already prepares impatiently for receiving the food. And so, your digestive organ already starts working while you are chewing.

The more your mouth is filled and the less you chew your food, the more saliva is produced by your body inharmoniously, which urges you to quickly swallow the half-chewed food that was inadequately supplied with saliva. The stomach, which perceives the disharmonious chewing movements in your pre-stomach, behaves in the same hectic manner as your teeth, palate and flow of saliva. For the saliva and the palate signal the aroma and quantity of the food arriving in the stomach, which now behaves in the same hectic way as your pre-stomach.

If the half-chewed, overly large quantity of food is swallowed, this gift of God will be processed by the gastric muscles and gastric juices in the same inharmonious way as by the teeth. Meanwhile, the palate is already demanding the next bite, which it also receives from the greed-driven person. The same process is repeated. The badly chewed food again slides into the stomach, which can no longer cope, being overtaxed. Hardly has the stomach received the half-chewed bite when the next bite is already being worked on in the person's mouth.

This continues until the person feels pressure in his stomach, through which the digestive organ signals to him: "Enough of that! I can no longer cope with my task of digesting everything." This pressure is indeed perceived by the human glutton, but what does he care? On top of everything, he drinks a glass of beer or wine, which he drinks as hastily as the food was gulped down.

The response to it all: Not only is the stomach overburdened, but all other organs connected with it are also affected. They are no longer capable of absorbing the food produced by the stomach in a hectic manner. They go on strike. Therefore, the food often remains in the body a very long time, producing gases that press on the organs and, above all, on the heart, burdening the whole organism.

Over the course of years, the activity of the stomach weakens. All other digestive organs also slacken: The liver, gallbladder, spleen and small and large intestines become lazy, due to the constant excessive activity. The heart and circulation are also influenced. The person becomes unattractively stout and often bloated, because the whole organism slackened prematurely. However, the person must continue attending to the duties of his occupation. This demands increased strength from his body. At first, he can still draw from his reserve strength. However, if it is used up, this or that organ will gradually become sick, having been continuously overtaxed, or several organs can become affected at the same time.

How does the unknowing, sick person react? He consults a doctor and complains about his pains and illnesses. The doctor prescribes medication for him and the one seeking healing takes it without hesitation. Without knowing that pharmaceutical medicine can harm more than help him, he takes it, hoping that he will soon become healthy again. While taking this medicine conscientiously, he complains to his family about his pains and illnesses. He describes his symptoms to his neighbors, his colleagues at work and his friends. Everyone feels sorry for him and wonders where these physical disruptive factors have come from, as he has indeed had a good life and certainly did not overexert himself physically. The person cannot recognize the causes and their correlations. And who should instruct him! Millions of people gobble up their meal greedily and do not know what causes their numerous complaints.

The Spirit of God has tried over and over again to enlighten humankind. He, the Lord, and His servants have revealed that every cause will have an effect. But humankind seldom listens to these admonishing voices coming from the spiritual realm.

Only some souls and people who have been prepared for this take the messages of the Spirit seriously. Others merely hear or read of them and put them aside. The great majority of people show no interest. They live for their day, indulging to their heart's content in only the things of an external life, until sooner or later the causes come into effect, either in this life or in a future one, perhaps flowing out into an earthly garment newly chosen by the soul. Every unlawful action creates a burden in the soul, since the magnetic-creative soul attracts the positive as well as the negative. Gluttony, craving for food and drink, hasty, uncontrolled eating are also sources of error, that is, causes, which burden the body as well as the soul.

Sanctify your food, for it is a gift from God!

In addition, the unknowing person, who seriously harms his body with excessive food and uncontrolled, hasty eating and drinking, greatly contributes to his cells becoming even more tired and his physical elasticity diminishing ever more – by his complaining and taking medicine.

However, the human being can program his brain and body cells with good, constructive vibrations as well as with negative ones. This means that he can transform himself downward even more with these negative vibrations. The person complains about his illness, about the heart, circulation, stomach, liver and gallbladder conditions, about being overweight and many other things.

O human being, accuse yourself! Your organs are not the originators of your illness. The originator is you, yourself, exclusively! Thus, the human being is to blame for his suffering. Neither does God send the illness, nor do the organs cause it. Solely the person's negative conduct is the source of error, nothing else. With continued negative thinking and acting, he damages his organism and at the same time, burdens his soul.

Every unlawful conduct toward God as well as toward the physical body burdens the soul. God gave to the human being a pure, cosmic soul. This soul is – just as He, the Lord – free of illness and suffering. It is solely the person, who, with his unlawful actions, incapacitates his soul in a cosmic sense for a long time, thus transforming down his body vibrations more and more each day.

Changing our thought
and practice into a God-conscious,
positive way of thinking and acting

If, O human being, after having read these revelations, you now decide for a life in accordance with the laws of the Lord, proceed as follows:

Remember that all that you have destroyed with many years of unlawful thinking, talking, and acting, cannot be restored again within a few days. Therefore, practice patience.

Sit on a chair, calmly and trustfully, but please, not in an easy chair. In reality, it is not comfortable at all for your skeleton or your whole body, although it may seem so. A chair that is too soft contributes to the deformation of your body. Therefore, sit on a chair, and place it so that you face east. In this way, your body is oriented to this direction, from which highly energetic powers flow to you, especially in the early morning hours. Assume an upright position; place the back of your hands on your thighs. Keep your head erect and close your eyes. Start with a brief analysis of your soul.

If you want to become healthy and peaceful, start to apply the spiritual medicine of your Inner Physician and Healer.

It is the Spirit of God in Christ, who knows about all things of life and who can put them in order, if you turn trustingly to Him.

So have confidence in Christ and believe in Him!

You have damaged your body, yourself, with a wrong way of thinking and acting. Repent of this and surrender all your impure sensations to Him, the great Physician and Healer in you.

Place everything that oppresses you on the fourth consciousness center, where the Christ-power, the consuming, healing flame burns.

Resolve to prepare your cell children, your body structure, with positive thoughts and words, by praying from your heart, something like the following:

> I ask you, O great Inner Physician, to stand by me! In me, in every cell of my body, is Your power. I affirm these powers.
> May they become effective in me.
> Everything that is impure in my soul and in my body, I lay at Your feet, You, the Inner Physician. I know that You will support me according to my

devotion, provided it is good for the salvation of my soul.

Continue in the following sense:
You are the strengthening power in me, which becomes more effective in every cell of my body from day to day.
I am the power of Your power.
I feel the refreshing fount of Your Holy Spirit. I now encourage my cell children, my cell structure, to drink from this fount.

Now direct your attention to the third consciousness center.

Then talk to your stomach or to one of the organs that are connected to this energy field.

Never tell an organ that it is sick.

Consider: If you never praise your child or never give it a present, but only reprimand it, then your child becomes listless and sad. It may suffer under depression or other setbacks.

Encourage your organs and praise them just as you do to your child as a good mother or father.

Tell your children, your cells and organs that a hidden power slumbers in them that you now want to awaken. They may drink from this inner fount of power. This inner power of God opens as soon as the person earnestly requests it. This is why this inner power should be invoked very consciously once or twice each day:

While you are sitting, completely relaxed, again and again direct your thoughts lovingly and appealingly toward the third consciousness center, which is in the lumbar region. From this energy field, the holy Spirit powers flow to your stomach, liver, spleen, small intestine, pancreas, to the spinal column and spinal cord. The healing powers disperse into the cells and organs awakened by you, giving them increased life. They eliminate sick and weak cells and stimulate the formation of new healthy ones. Proceed in this way with your body each day, and you will feel tangible relief.

In doing so, it is very important that you change your eating habits. Eat little food from animals, but more grains, fruits and vegetables. Drink good fruit and vegetable juices, preferably pressed by yourself. Make it your habit to take only small bites; chew them well and slowly. Drink in small sips and set the cup or glass down after every sip. While doing all this, raise your spirit to God. Be aware of the fact that God's power is effective in all life forms, also in the food you eat. Thus, sanctify your food! All you do and achieve should be with God in mind. He, the Lord, whose Spirit is in you and whose child you are, wants only the best for you.

These God-conscious actions will bring your stomach to a genuine activity again. It will work more joyfully, since the food was chewed well and the quantity is less. The stomach will supply the substance of the food to the cells and organs, which were addressed by you and are thus willing to work.

O human being, try to reduce the intake of medication, as well. While asking for the ether powers, slowly adapt your body to natural remedies. Natural remedies are also merely an aid for your body, which has not yet oriented itself completely to the healing ether powers. The medicinal plants or their potencies are not harmful for your organs, since they are in harmony with the ether streams.

Be patient with yourself. Do not become impatient, even if it takes a very long time before the Inner Physician and Healer can become fully effective. Consider how long you have been acting against His power, thus suppressing it. Activate this divine healing power now, by turning to Christ and by leading a lawful life, by refining yourself and developing upbuilding, high thoughts and words. Be on your guard against unlawfulness. Through a few impure thoughts, words and actions, you can quickly destroy what you have built up for your body during days of good will. Practice, and base everything you do on the standard of the Spirit. Use moderation in everything and be conscious of the presence of God with every single action. This strengthens your body and your soul, so that some day you will not lack anything, because God is your standard in everything and you have become His conscious child.

Through your way of thinking and acting, you can influence all the organs of your body in a positive or in a negative manner.

Recognize, O human being, from what energy field of your body which organs receive the holy ether powers.

As revealed already, the stomach, liver, spleen, small intestine, and pancreas, among others, are supplied by the third consciousness center. The kidneys with the ureters, the rectum and the large intestine, among others, are supplied by the second consciousness center, which is located in the area of the sacrum.

The ether power, the life from God, flows in all Being. As I explained, all the organs mentioned above can be addressed. The prerequisite, however, is that the person completely change his life and entrust himself to the Inner Physician more than to external medical skills.

Often an operation is unavoidable. In case this has to be done, do not despair! Your life lies in God's hands.

Spheres of purification and incarnations – Their significance for the development of the soul

Many people think that external influences, for instance, operations or dangerous encounters with aggressive people, can prematurely terminate one's life on Earth.

Consider, O human being: The course of your life is initially determined by the radiation picture of your soul, which chooses for an incarnation the corresponding planetary constellation, that is, its influence on the person.

Every person is thus born under a certain constellation. This is nothing more than a concentration of certain kinds of radiations, which continue to influence the soul and the person until he has developed beyond the effects of these planets.

According to his way of life, a person can develop to a higher state of consciousness than the one he brought with him, or he can fall back into a lower one. All these tendencies are evident in the radiation picture of the soul and in the constellation.

There are schools in the spheres of the beyond, just as on this Earth. In these schools, the souls are taught about cosmic facts and correlations. Spirit beings, that is, angel teachers, especially care for those souls that are striving for a further incarnation. It is essential for these souls to know what to expect in the earthly garment. If a soul follows the instructions of its angel teacher, this soul is allowed to look into the approaching radiation field of its constellation, in order to become acquainted with the various possibilities of its life's course in a human body. This picture of the planetary constellation discloses itself to the soul and shows possible approaching blows of fate. The soul, which is willing to incarnate, can see its tendencies and inclinations toward the positive and as well as the negative. Both are visible in the constellation of the soul.

Often, a soul will see its extremely strong inclination toward the negative, thus recognizing what difficult situations and blows of fate could take place when it is in the earthly garment. Such a soul is advised in the spirit school to abstain from a further incarnation. Those appointed to teach the soul recommend that it remain in the soul realms to improve its condition, until its radiation picture shows more positive aspects. The development of the soul can also be accomplished in the soul realms. It is easier to improve the radiation picture of the soul there, than in a physical body. There is such great ignorance about these correlations prevailing among you human beings that I want to reveal some more fundamental aspects:

The state of consciousness of every soul can be recognized by the nuances of color in the soul's garments. If these colors differ widely from celestial law radiations, the details of the soul's guilt can be distinctly recognized. Every spirit being, including the angel teachers, can make the condition of the soul's garments visible in pictures. Therefore, looking at itself and within itself, the soul can recognize the blows of fate and troubles that will come to it in an earthly garment. Also partly apparent in this soul image is the detailed guidance by the planetary constellation, whose power influences are identical with the state of the soul wanting to incarnate. In this process, the soul recognizes that if several nuances of color in its soul garments were to become lighter, then this or that blow of fate, which would otherwise cause great pain and misery on Earth and hinder its spiritual development, would fall from the soul once it is incarnated.

A soul, willing to incarnate and that believes in this inner vision shown by the angel teacher and that is striving to purify more quickly on Earth than in the soul realms, can attend a special spiritual schooling. The souls willing to incarnate are instructed there as to how they can improve their soul image more quickly while in the earthly garment. They receive detailed instructions and guidance, so that the soul's garments become more light-filled and the soul's tendency, that is, its vibration, is raised. On their way to incarnation, these souls do go via the constellation that is equal to their soul image. But the soul enters a higher radiation field of this constellation, which has more positive aspects. In this way, the incarnated soul is offered the possibility, while in the earthly garment and over the course of years, to raise itself from this radiation field into the next higher one, which, considering everything, would not have been possible so quickly in the soul realms.

However, if a soul is already in the third or even the fourth consciousness level – that is, in the third or fourth astral or purification sphere, better in the third or fourth purification plane – because in former incarnations on Earth it completed a more intense path of purification, then it senses precisely that a more rapid development to higher levels may be possible in the soul realms than in still more incarnations. The soul's tendency is the decisive factor here, too. For instance: If a soul is on the third level of consciousness and its spiritual tendencies already project into the fourth level, then its garments are already more light-filled than those of a soul which could just barely qualify for this third level, but has reached this plane of development or purification only recently and still shows tendencies of the second consciousness level.

These spiritual laws vary greatly, because everything is based on radiation and nuances of color, making it impossible to describe this in detail. Every soul must be guided individually, until it has put away its individuality, its own independent thoughts, and has become one with the Infinite.

As soon as the soul has put on its earthly garment, its past is covered up. If a soul undergoes a spiritual schooling in the realms of the beyond until it has attained a corresponding development of its garments, it will be much easier for the soul to follow positive aspects when in an earthly garment and to improve its soul image, or even to develop out of it. The result is that higher vibrating forces influence the soul, and thus, its life on Earth can be more peaceful and harmonious.

An operation – Turning point and opportunity in the life of a human being

When a person is faced with surgery during his life on Earth, it could be he is facing a turning point that can lead him to a higher development. This means that he can influence the radiation picture of his soul positively or negatively. An operation can be the moment in your life at which you can – depending on the radiation picture of your soul – set out on a negative path, or, by praying and turning to God and the divine laws, on a positive one. There are high points set in every human life, through which the person and its soul can awaken to a higher self, if he recognizes these crossroads in his life and if he decides for the positive, that is, for the divine and the divine laws. This means that surgery can bring about a turning point in a human life.

However, many people do not recognize this possibility for changing their direction in life.

Soul and person could attain a higher vibration through a successful operation. If the person does not recognize this pointer of his fate, he can suddenly slide away from a good way and reach a direction that goes away from God, our Lord. With this, further negative events can enter his life. Therefore, the attitude one has before undergoing surgery is very important. Every operation is an intrusion into your physical life as well as into your spiritual spheres. Every medicine has a negative effect on the vibrations of the ether body.

Therefore, O human being, strive to pray deeply to God and to commend yourself to God, before you undergo an operation your doctor has recommended. If you have aligned your life to the divine laws, God will lead you to this operation, protect the ether body and give the necessary impulses to the physician. Every serious operation can be a guide for you, because it is also predetermined by the constellation and is under its influence. If you tend toward God by living according to His laws, the operation will be successful, either for the benefit of your soul or for soul and body. Therefore, leave your fate to God and surrender your life to Him.

Do not have fearful thoughts before the operation. In doing this, you send out vibrations that can, among other things, influence the surgeon and affect him. In addition, your body will become tense. Even if you are given relaxing medication, it does not loosen the tension in your soul caused by fearful thoughts. As long as the soul is tense, through days of worry and fear, it will give little life force, that is, ether powers, to the physical body. These powers are then lacking in your organs.

The result can be varied. For example, the physician cannot diagnose the actual cause of the disease, since an organ, deprived of the cosmic life force, often seems to be more ill than it really is. Or you feel a pain that originates in an illness that is actually harmless. Your excessive anxiety that a serious illness could exist makes you more and more tense and the pain increases. In your excessive anxiety, you then go to the doctor who may recommend an operation that is not absolutely necessary.

Such and similar wrong decisions can lead you onto an unlawful path, which is indicated in your constellation as a crossroads toward the negative. Faulty reactions can lead the soul and person onto a downhill path, so that the operation will be unsuccessful, or merely seem to be successful, resulting in further difficulties later on. Everything is indicated in your life picture, in your soul, and in your constellation.

Your fate lies in your hand

Many souls taught in the spheres of purification do not listen to the angel teachers' admonitions and instructions. They incarnate at the next possible planetary constellation, that is, when the inclinations of their soul are addressed by one of the seven times seven cosmic rays.

And so, your fate, O human being, lies in your hand. Your positive as well as your negative characteristics and inclinations emanate from you, from your soul. They do not come from God, who is beyond human inclinations.

A person who knows the laws of the Lord will place his fate in the hands of God and, through the ether powers flowing perpetually to him, make the best of his life. People could avert many things from themselves, if they knew the inherent laws of life. However, they must then also apply them.

Therefore, O human being, do not become tense immediately upon feeling pain, and do not immediately fear the worst. What is terrible in your life? Only that which you caused yourself, as a result of your ignorance of the spiritual laws and through your negative way of thinking and acting. A person is the sole originator of his fate. The causes determining your fate can lie far back. Everything is openly shown in your soul image. These records concern the deeds from your previous lives, which may now come into effect in your present physical life span.

During its life here on Earth, a soul that listened to the instructions of the angel teachers can be more easily influenced toward the positive via the conscience, by its guardian spirit or its inner guide, the Holy Spirit, than a disobedient soul that incarnated under mostly negative aspects. But this soul is also given the possibility to change its ways, although it cannot recognize this so easily and cannot always understand and actualize what it is called upon to do by the Spirit. And so, the one who knows these deeper spiritual laws and correlations of cause and effect should also apply this knowledge correctly. However, someone who knows but little of these laws of the Lord and their interconnections cannot plead ignorance. For one thing, he knows the excerpts of the law of God, the commandments, and secondly, he has already frequently heard the words of Jesus: "A person will reap what he sows."

Conduct before surgery

Provided immediate surgery is not necessary – as with severe injuries of the arteries, appendicitis, broken legs, and so forth – go into the stillness first. Assume the Christian meditation position, as already revealed, and turn trustingly to God, our Lord, your Father.

If possible, and especially in summer, sit at sunrise by an open window or in your garden, a field or in the woods. There, assume the aforementioned meditation position, facing east. Breathe in the ether powers flowing down on you from the cosmos and, while breathing, link with the Lord, your God, whose Spirit dwells in your soul. Ask Him for guidance and help for your life. Filled with trust, open yourself to Him and be patient. Let go of subliminal thoughts of the operation, even in the deep layers of your brain, in your subconscious. Free yourself from any anxiety and pray from deep in your heart to the One who knows all things and can guide everything. Trust Him and surrender yourself completely to Him.

Once you have attained deep calmness, guide the ether energies, which are healing powers, to your painful areas by way of your thoughts – which are powers, as you have now frequently heard. Open yourself completely to these healing powers and – as it has been revealed again and again in this book – talk to the respective organs or cells. You can talk to all the parts of your body, to the kidneys, the ureters and your rectum and large intestine. In all of your organs, including the nerves, glands and hormones, the Divine, the ether power, is waiting to unfold.

However, consider that when you ask for the holy powers, it is also necessary that your life, that is, your thoughts and actions, be in the spirit of the divine laws. Do not talk about your pain unless you feel the need to seriously share this with one of your neighbors. Before you do so, pray to the inner guide, the Spirit. Ask Him to guide you and to be your spokesman in the impending conversation. The Lord of your soul will then lead you – if it is His will – to a person who can perhaps help you by way of an herb or with a corresponding instruction for your life. Do not, however, complain of your suffering to your neighbor, but explain your situation to him with something like the following statement of faith: "Everything lies in His hands. I let myself be instructed and guided by Him, my Lord."

When in your meditation, you invoke the ether powers, direct your thoughts to the fourth consciousness center, which is between your shoulder blades, near the heart. Ask the Redeemer-light that is effective there for inner guidance and for increased ether powers. Then direct your sensations and thoughts to the second field of power, from which the healing streams flow for your large intestine, rectum and ureter, among others. Ask for increased life powers for the sick organ. Speak with this organ and, with life-affirming thoughts, encourage it to orient itself to the inner, healing ether powers.

If the organs addressed by you have received too much medicine, then they are oriented to without. Their cells rely on the administered medicine. Therefore, slowly reduce these medications and make your cells and organs understand that they also receive the healing gifts from the Inner Physician and Healer. Speak to them in the following sense:

From the eternal wellspring, which alone can give you the best medicine, you receive now, dear kidney (or: you, large intestine, etc.), the upbuilding powers.

Turn now to the Inner Physician and Healer. Do not listen to the desires of your body for earthly medicine, which are signaling to you via the stomach or via the blood. Listen to the holy and healing ether power. Open yourself to the medicine from the eternal wellspring of all Being.

You cells, open your mouths and drink the auspicious powers. Spirit flows to spirit, God's power to God's power, divine love to the love for God, for like attracts like.

Now, speak further heartfelt words to the sick organs. Know that the Inner Physician is the life in all Being, and thus, in every cell of your body, as well.

Often, an operation would not be necessary if, in his life, the person had the correct attitude toward the divine.

When you walk the path to God with God, your Lord in Christ, then change your eating and drinking habits, as well. Refrain from foods that are very spicy. The vibrations of these spices affect your soul unpleasantly, touching the ether powers, which then withdraw. Avoid nicotine and alcohol and reduce animal food more and more, above all, meat and fish. Abstain entirely from drugs. They unimaginably burden the ether body, the soul of the person, and, sooner or later, can lead to death, since the ether powers withdraw more and more, and the soul can thus no longer maintain and support its body.

Lead a life that is in the will of God. Then, you will find your way to the positive path of life, which is recorded in your soul image. Through this turnabout toward the good in your life, you awaken the holy ether powers, which will guide and instruct you. Keep following this path of evolution that you have now begun. Practice good and benevolent thinking and acting. In your daily life, try to stay in contact with God, the inner light of your soul, by proving to be a child of your heavenly Father and sending Him thoughts of love during the day, wherever you may be. Try to go within several times a day, and be aware of His guiding hand.

If you learn that an operation is unavoidable, then turn to the All-One again and ask for His guidance. Go trustingly to the operation. You are now well prepared, physically and mentally.

On the day of the operation go into meditation again, wherever you might be, in bed in your hospital room or in the anteroom of the operating room. Talk to your Inner Physician and Healer, to Christ, the helping and healing power in you, and then with your sick organ. Encourage your blood circulation in the same way as you have learned to address the cells and organs of your body, in order to bring them into harmony.

Surrender yourself completely into the hands of the Inner Physician. Then, His radiation, which is flowing through you, can guide the surgeon. When you receive the first injection for the anesthetization of your consciousness, look at this narcotic briefly, place your blessing thoughts on the content of the syringe, and, at the same time, bless the doctor or the assistant who is treating you. Bless the whole operation team. Then, pray until you fall asleep.

The will of God will then be done in you. He, your Father, the light and power in you, and in all people, wants only the best for you and for all His children. He thinks first of the eternal substance, your soul. According to His lawful criteria, you will receive His helping powers.

Regardless of how the operation went, remain on this path of trust in God and do not allow anything or anybody to dissuade you from this path of love for Him. Know that you are a child of the All-Highest. Your Father, who is all-embracing love, knows how to guide His child so that the child can – after the struggle of this life – victoriously reach the arms of its Father. Therefore, do not let up, and remain untiringly on the path to eternal life. No matter what you may encounter as joy or sorrow, and no matter what may hit you, remain trustingly oriented solely to Him, your Lord.

Even though ever so many obstacles and hurdles may be put in your way, think of your soul image, of your constellation. All hurdles and obstacles must withdraw from it. Do not forget: Deferred is not cancelled. Everything that is impure must be recognized and brought to Him, the Absolute, the One, so that your soul image becomes free of all human negativity. Only with a daily, positive work on yourself will you reach the lawful evolution that will bring you nearer to God, your Father. Thus, your life should be the march of victory over your self.

The first consciousness center: Coccyx area

The breath of the Holy Spirit respirates and maintains every human being. The more a person turns to God, his eternal Father, with all his aspirations, the more Spirit power flows into his soul and into the physical body. The breath of the Holy Spirit, also called ether or life force, which can pulsate through the soul and physical body more intensely with its holy powers, gives harmony and joy to the fine-ethereal as well as the coarse-material body. This results in health for all the cells and organs of your body. This process takes place via the cell membranes. The more harmoniously and balanced they vibrate, the healthier the cells are, and thus, the more balanced and free the person becomes.

Such a spiritualized person, whose sole aspiration is to strive toward the eternal Holy Spirit, will not be content with inadequate worldly opinions and ideas. He knows about the eternally true and fundamental law of life, which is: All cosmically pure powers are in me. A person who has turned within knows the inherent laws of God, which are healing, vivifying and maintaining energetic powers for the soul as well as the coarse-material body. A person of the Spirit, a true child of God, also knows how to apply these powers. This is why the Lord said, in effect: Become perfect, as your Father in heaven is perfect.

Therefore, if the eternal law of God flows in a person, he may also address it, on condition that he knows about these cosmic correlations. He must also recognize that these holy powers will become increasingly active only if he lives according to this flowing law and does not reduce it more and more with negative thoughts and actions. If the person does not come into harmony with this inner law, the inner light, the ether power, will recede. Consequently, it will grow ever darker in his physical body. The result is that the person thus "forges his own fate": His impure conduct can bring him insurmountable hurdles in this life that build a further guilt in the soul, a karma.

Thus, once the holy Spirit powers become active in a God-filled person and he knows the spiritual healing method, he can invoke the divine healing powers via the already revealed centers.

It is, in effect, written: "Ask, and it will be given to you. Seek and you will find. Knock, and it will be opened to you." As already revealed, a person may knock at the first consciousness center, the energy field of Order, to which the following organs are connected: the pelvic area with the hip joints, sexual organs, uterus with ovaries, oviducts, vagina, prostate gland, seminal gland with spermatic duct, penis and bladder. All these organs may now be addressed in the manner revealed, by the one seeking healing who turns to spiritual self-healing:

O human being, now assume the Christian meditation posture and link with your God and Lord, your inner Guide. Think about your life and repent of your faults and weaknesses that you have recognized, for the Lord said in essence: "Go forth and sin no more." This means: What you have recognized and repented of, you should not call back again anymore, neither in thoughts, nor in words, nor in actions.

Provided you have placed into God's hands your weaknesses that you have earnestly repented of and have resolved to sin no more, your inner life powers will immediately intensify. Already after a short time, you will feel the powers of the Spirit that are flowing to you.

Now ask again for help, relief or healing. Then, turn your thoughts to the weak or sick organ. With your will, which is devoted to God, now guide the healing ether powers to the sickly organs by way of the power and might of your thoughts that are turned to God. Talk to these cell structures, because in each cell is the holy ether power, the Spirit.

With impure, unlawful thoughts and actions, to a large extent you have repressed these powers of God in the innermost part of your cells. Address these cells now, by sending them upbuilding, highly vibrating thoughts.

For instance, if you, a woman, suffer from the inflammation of the ovaries, or if you, a man, have prostate problems, say, in effect:

You, my abdominal organ, listen: From without and from within, the healing gifts of grace now flow to you. Open yourself to the powers of the Inner Physician and Healer. Now, accept my good sensations and thoughts, too, which are meant for you. In the entire cosmic life, there is neither fatigue nor illness. In the spheres from which you now receive the healing powers, everything is eternally active power.

Now, I have learned that thoughts are mighty powers, in the positive as well as in the negative sense.

What you, my organ, are lacking is encouragement, so that your cells can turn to the divine life force, which I now ask for daily more and more, by living a life that is in the will of God.

You cells, open your mouths now, and drink from the beneficial power.

I affirm the health in me. Fatigue recedes from my whole body. The holy powers move in and the sick cells leave my body. I repeat: The holy powers move in and the sick cells leave my body. New and healthy cells are born.

I repeat: New and healthy cells in my body are born!

The Spirit is active in my abdominal organs.

I repeat: the Spirit is active in my abdominal organs (for instance, uterus, prostate gland, and the like).

Repeat these short appeals to your sick organ frequently during the day, wherever you might be. In this way, you program the cells of your brain and body, and simultaneously activate the ether power, the Spirit, the life force in you.

Do not forget, however, to go into stillness at least once a day, at best, in the morning, in order to connect most closely to God, your Lord, so that He, the Infinite, can guide you during the course of your day.

Do everything with God, your Lord, and strive to lead a lawful life. Pay attention to all the instructions given in this book, so that each of your seven consciousness centers is activated via the tree of life, and all your organs can be permeated by the holy ether powers flowing from the healing wellspring of the power of the Christ of God.

Practice patience, for you have sinned for many years, often, even in your previous lives, over which a veil lies, as desired by God. All these still existing shadows must be permeated with light so that your weak and sick organs can drink abundantly of the vital powers of the Spirit.

You ask: "Why has the Lord put a veil over my past?" A person should not think about his past, so that he not waste valuable time during his present life on Earth. Know that God is omniscient and also knows your past. This should be enough for you.

In your present earthly existence, devote yourself completely, thankfully and trustingly, to God, your Father and Lord. He, the All-One, knows what you are lacking. In His boundless love, He will support you and will put everything in order for you.

Devotion to God is the most important aspect for your becoming healthy. Furthermore, you have to live in accordance with the laws of God, so that the Spirit power can be fulfilled in you.

People say that God, our Lord, has grown an herb for every illness. Know that the many herbs are a manifested level of evolution from the thoughts of God. From the divine ether powers, which consist of various degrees of vibration, the mineral, plant and animal kingdoms came forth, as well as the set ether potencies, the nature beings, which consist of all spiritually cosmic components of infinity, but which were not yet raised to the filiation in God.

The eternally existing ether body of the perfect spirit beings emerged from these spiritual-energetic joinings of the individual vibration powers of the divine ether. This pure spirit body is called soul in its sevenfold, shadowed shell.

Recognize, O human being: The components of the herbs are thus in you as vibration and are also in the ether power, the healing power of God, which flows throughout all your soul particles and body cells, providing them with life force, and thus, maintaining them alive. Therefore, all trace elements that your body needs are contained in the divine ether powers.

God's manifested thoughts of evolution, the herbs, which you take as tea or in a potentiated form, are given to you by the Spirit of life, because the sensations and thoughts of human beings have been preoccupied with ideas and things that do not correspond to the divine laws, thus distancing themselves more and more from God, the flowing ether power.

The entire creation is in you!

The powers of each little herb, of each trace element, of every vitamin, that is, everything that your body needs, you can receive from the divine ether powers that are flowing constantly through you, provided these holy powers can become fully effective and active in you through a lawful life. Everything is based on radiation; everything is energy. Matter is nothing but transformed, lowly-vibrating crystallized ether.

The one who raises his soul to the higher powers receives them for his soul as well as for his body.

You can apply such positive, highly vibrating thoughts of invocation, which activate the holy ether powers in you, to all your organs, cells, hormones, glands and limbs.

If you take a lot of medication, I, Brother Emanuel, the inspirer of this divine knowledge, recommend that you reduce this medicine and gradually switch to natural products. These gifts of salvation are in harmony with the divine ether, as you have now learned.

As you have gathered from this revelation, teas made from various herbs are also recommended by the Spirit of God for healing and strengthening, since the ether powers are not fully effective in most people.

For instance, when you, a woman, suffer from an abdominal illness (uterus), prepare yourself a tea made of white dead nettle, lesser centaury, yarrow, coltsfoot and stinging nettle. Combine these herbs in equal parts and drink the tea lukewarm, in sips, two or three cups spread over the day. If possible, do not add sugar. If you want to sweeten this salutary drink, use a half to one teaspoon of wild honey, or the same quantity of fruit sugar, but no more.

The Spirit places great value on the spiritual healing methods in this revelation, as suggested by the title of this book. This is why I only occasionally reveal various kinds of tea mixtures and other natural healing methods.

If you, a man, have complaints of the abdominal organs (of the prostate gland), for example, I recommend tea of silverweed, lovage, willow herb, plantain, lawn daisy, oxlip or key flower, wild chicory and a small quantity of alder buckhorn bark. Blend these kinds of teas in the same way as mentioned above and drink in sips.

For women with abdominal complaints, I recommend as follows:

Hip baths every other day, made of oak bark or fresh savory. Take five handfuls or a big bunch of savory and bring to a boil and let simmer for approximately two minutes. Then strain and add to the bath water. Take the hip bath for about ten minutes, then dry off the body and keep it good and warm.

For strengthening the weak abdominal organs or for healing inner ulcers, rubdowns of the abdomen with oak bark or savory preparations are advantageous. Prepare the extract of oak bark in good non-carbonated mineral water in a cobalt-blue vessel. Savory should be put into alcohol.

Place the open bowl containing these natural products in the morning sun, four to five times approximately, when the sun is shining. The bowl should be brought back into the room by 10 AM at the latest, and left covered in the room. After 4-5 days, the abdomen can be rubbed daily with this extract.

In addition, drink daily two cups of a tea made of lady mantle, bedstraw, plantain and orchid. Drink it spread throughout the day, lukewarm and in sips, for approximately four weeks. After this time, change the tea: take a small amount of columbine, tormentil, yarrow and silverweed.

It is very important to always keep the abdomen warm. Wear garments made exclusively of natural fibers. In this way, a positive charging of the body's magnetic field is brought about and the body of the person seeking healing is charged positively.

Summary of the wisdom vital for healing body and soul

I will now summarize the wisdom that is vital for healing your soul and body:

The inexhaustible powers of the Spirit, the holy law, the ether powers, open to every human being in their infinite diversity. The entire creative life, God, the ether power, flows in every soul and in every physical body.

Every creative sensation of the Holy Spirit flows through the body as soothing, strengthening and healing power, as spiritual ether in soul and person. The holy, active ether powers are contained in the mineral, plant and animal kingdoms. This divine power potential can also become fully effective in the soul and person. The ether powers of the Infinite are the Spirit of God, the eternally flowing law.

The more a person turns to God, his Father, and fulfills His law, the more intensely the ether powers, also called healing powers, flow in the soul and body.

So that you can lead a lawful life, which builds up the powers of the Spirit in you and makes them flow more intensely, it is necessary that you heed the following fundamental spiritual truths:

The most important aspect in the life of a person are positive, upbuilding sensations, thoughts and words.

Your body is like a sounding board: Every ignoble and negative thought triggers negative vibrations in this sounding board, which spread out not only over your whole body, but also over your soul.

Recognize: When you throw a stone into the water, it creates circles. The same happens when you send out positive or negative sensations, thoughts, and words.

The sounding board, your body, and your soul vibrate in the same way as you feel, think and act. With high vibrations, which your noble feelings, inclinations and thoughts bring forth, you contribute to the purification of your soul and the illumination of your organism. This means that the higher your soul vibrates, the more intensely the holy powers of God flow in you.

Every unlawful thought and act disturbs the spiritual law in the human being. This means that the ether powers withdraw, because they cannot flow parallel to low human vibrations.

Become accustomed to speaking slowly and harmoniously. Say only essential and positive things. Do not even take in anything that is not essential. It reduces your spiritual and physical powers and contributes to disharmony.

*Daily preparation of the soul
in the morning*

A person cleanses and cares for his body every morning. He should cleanse his soul in the same manner each morning. Therefore, O human being, pray when you first awaken. Then get up in good time, and wash and dress yourself. Afterward, it would be good to do light, rhythmic, physical exercises.

These light exercises, which contribute to the preparation of your soul and to the loosening of your body, were conveyed to the prophetess through the spiritual inner vision. These spiritual, physical exercises are taught in the first and second meditation courses of Jesus Christ. The exercises in the first meditation course are preparatory exercises. In the second meditation course, more intense exercises are taught, which have an increased effect on the soul and the physical body, but, above all, on the person's consciousness centers.

As soon as you have done light body exercises and your meditation, which contributes to internalization, have breakfast in absolute harmony.

If you still have time, program your brain cells with highly vibrating words. Your brain cells will transmit these programmed thoughts directly to the cells, organs, glands, hormones, and to your whole body structure.

Speak in the following sense:
All positive powers are in me.
My soul and my body align with the helpful, guiding and healing powers.
God is eternal harmony. I am eternal harmony. The hectic ways of this world do not touch me, for I am eternal harmony.
I am the love and the wisdom from God's omnipotence and greatness.
All ignoble feelings and base inclinations that want to overwhelm me, I surrender to the almighty Spirit in me.
I am spirit.
May my words be vivified by God's breath, so that I say only what is in the will of God, for I am spirit. The Spirit of my Father is in me.
I am His child.
His radiant Spirit cares for me. Therefore, I am constantly in Him, and He, the light, dwells in me. I

am healthy because His healing power and love irradiate and strengthen me.

His upbuilding power is in me.

In and with God, my Father in Christ, I start my daily work.

Peace and love to all people and souls, who are my brothers and sisters.

Unity and creative love be with all life forms, with the mineral, plant and animal kingdoms.

His life is in all things, in the sun as well as in the moon and the stars.

I affirm the material as well as the spiritual creation.

I affirm the eternal presence of God, His eternally, harmoniously loving Spirit, which flows throughout all Being.

I live eternally.

My eternal body knows neither time nor space. I am eternal existence, eternal Being.

I am spirit.

*How can I keep my soul and body
in harmony?*

O human being, make it a habit to sanctify your meals and to take them in peace and quiet. Put aside haste and hectic activity. Eat highly vibrating food and eat only a little. Take small portions and chew them well. Drink moderately and in small sips.

Walk harmoniously and uprightly. The spiritually wise person recognizes the state of your soul by your gestures as well as your movements. Become accustomed to gesticulating and walking in a harmonious manner.

All these behavioral indications contribute to internalizing and harmonizing your soul and body.

With constant self-observation, and a positive, lawful programming of your subconscious, you will awaken to becoming a spiritual person who knows how to direct the ether powers according to the law of the Lord.

Do not be afraid, God dwells and works in you! Fear and anxiety have a negative effect on your soul and disturb the flow of the holy powers in you.

Link frequently during the day with your heavenly Father, whose Spirit dwells in you.

Be sparing with the intake of medications. They consume the energy and have a disharmonizing effect on the ether body in you and on your physical body. If you cannot get along without medications, ask God, your Lord, to bless them. He, the Spirit in you, can largely neutralize the harmful ingredients. However, the blessing of this medicine becomes effective only when you recognize the medicine as a disturbing factor for your soul and for your physical body and are willing to work on yourself in order to reeducate your body.

Avoid loud and disharmonious music. It disturbs your well-being and diminishes the vibration of your soul.

Rhythmical music also disturbs your general condition. It can even trigger soul burdens that can directly affect your soul and your body.

Harmonious music, on the other hand, contributes to harmonizing your soul and your physical body, as well.

Never forget to thank God for His blessings and prove yourself to be an obedient child that, by way of self-analysis and actualization of the divine laws in its daily life, works on itself, thus becoming selfless and willing to make sacrifices. God can then give you all His love, wisdom, and strength even more tangibly.

PART 3

Futher Instructions and Recommendations Concerning Certain Illnesses

Increased performance and equilibrium by positively charging the magnetic field

A targeted magnetic charging of the soul and body brings about a healing success and increased performance, among other things. A positive magnetic field also results in balance and harmony.

With the help of a quartz stone we can strengthen our spiritual-physical magnetic field. Proceed as follows:

Place the quartz stone under flowing water for half an hour. Then rub it in the palms of your hands for five minutes. Subsequently, put it in your pocket as a magnetic charging field for your body.

You can proceed with a silver ring in a similar way, in which a quartz, amber or aquamarine is set. Place the ring under flowing water for fifteen minutes, then rub it between the palms of your hands for five minutes. Then put it on your ring finger. These stones, set in silver, can also be worn on a silver necklace.

Charging the stones with magnetic power as described here, using water and by rubbing them between the palms, should be repeated every four days.

Conduct when feeling fatigue, depression and loss of energy

If a person is always tired or suffers from depression, which often triggers aggression as well, he should go to a waterfall as often as possible. There, he should sit at the edge of the water and watch the lively and sparkling water falling and bubbling over the stones. In doing this, the person frees himself from his depressive and tormenting thoughts.

By constantly striking the stones, the water develops very strong magnetic powers, which the tired, stressed, apathetic, aggressive and depressed person absorbs.

Every despondency is a sign of loss of energy, which cannot always be compensated with good, highly vibrating nutrition. Often, charging the spiritual-physical magnetic field is necessary in the manner mentioned above. This should mainly be done during the early summer and the summer months, at sunrise or during the early morning, until approximately 10 AM.

If a person is charged with too much energy, especially after a hot sunny day that he had to spend under solar radiation, he should let cold or cool water flow down the arms, from the elbows down the arms and over the back of the hands, but not over the palms. In this way, the energy will be carried off. You gain the same effect by a cool stream of water. Let it flow down for approximately two minutes from the hollow of the knees over the calves and heels down to the soles of the feet. This also carries off the energy.

Intense solar radiation and the accumulation of heat can also cause a lack of energy in some people. Among other things, it can lead to a drop in blood circulation. The following is advisable for this:

Drink light, lukewarm tea with lemon, in sips, not all at once. Teas made of silverweed, rosemary or apple, with lemon or orange have the same effect.

*The frequencies of the ocean waves
increase the vitality of the body
and the life forces of the soul*

High energetic forces are also radiated by the ocean waves onto the mainland, especially during the morning hours when the tide comes in. These forces come from the deepest depths of the ocean. When the depths of the ocean come into strong movement through the sun's irradiation, energetic forces of silver, manganese, copper and many other elements flow toward the mainland. The one who consciously aligns with these energetic forces and their high frequencies can refresh his spiritual and physical energy deficiency and his entire physical functioning, since these high gifts of life correct an often existing deficiency of trace elements.

*Why older people
like to feed birds*

Especially flying animals neutralize strong fields of tension by their vibration. Older people, who often have a spiritual and physical energy deficiency, perceive this smoothing of tensions and like to go into this relaxing force field, which balances their energy – depending on their attitude and level of consciousness.

*General indications
for the illness of cancer*

When suffering from cancer, especially lung cancer, it is advisable to drink tea made of very young shoots of spruce, which still bear the morning dew and thus, high ether powers. Soak these shoots in good, non-carbonated mineral water for one to two hours. Then bring it to a boil for a short time. Drink two to three cups during the day, lukewarm, in sips and not sweetened. Mud or clay baths can also have a soothing or healing effect on cancer. Cancer can develop in many ways.

There is also a disordered growth of cells (cancer) that is triggered exclusively by fear or by tension in the nervous system and the cell structure.

Cancer of the blood, for instance, can also be hereditary. It can be healed if the person changes his way of life entirely. The person must change not only his way of thinking, but also his way of eating. It would be advisable to drink at lot of freshly squeezed plant juices, vegetable juices and apple juice. Drinking rather than eating more of these qualities, will cleanse – or better said, renew – the blood. The patient should abstain from all alcoholic drinks, nicotine and all salted food. He should also avoid artificial fragrances, for instance, sprays, perfumes and so forth. Furthermore, it would be advisable not to partake of any meat, sausage and cold cuts or fish, nor fried or strongly spiced food. Also, roux and everything that contains fat should be avoided.

These are all merely suggestions. The Spirit and the brothers and sisters serving Him cannot, of course, guarantee soothing or healing effects. God's healing powers from the plants and from nature are given to every individual according to the will of the Lord and the person's spiritual development. The Lord of life cares for the welfare of the soul, above all, and then for the physical body.

The healing effects of rye and wheat fields

People suffering from asthma and illnesses of the thyroid gland, lungs, nerves, abdomen and cancer should walk through a field of rye or wheat at sunrise, and while walking, be very consciously aligned with God's power. The ears of grain willingly release the ether powers, the sun and moon particles that they have absorbed in abundance.

For hay fever, put fresh hay with many blossoms into a linen cloth and put it under your pillow. The effect would be more lasting if you would sleep directly on this linen bag. During the day, frequently smell freshly dried marjoram, which you, at best, sew into a handkerchief.

With the awakening of the ether powers, these measures contribute to relieving or curing hay fever.

With anorexia, one should take care to strengthen his nerves. In this way, the thyroid gland is also stabilized. Dishes of rice, wheat, oats, and barley will hasten the healing. Apples also strengthen the nerves and should be eaten several times a day. They should be chewed very well. It would be best to grate them.

The ether powers of various kinds of moss and of forest grass

The ether powers, which present themselves in manifold ways, can also be received from the following life forms:

Moss growing in the forest stimulates fertility. Moss growing in the garden strengthens the heart and stomach.

Sit or stand on these mosses when the sun is shining, facing the sun, and consciously breathe in and absorb the highly energetic powers of the moss.

Next to coniferous trees, most of the ether powers cling to the grass of the forest. In the morning, when the sun rises and shines on the grass, lie on the grass in the forest, wrapped in a thin linen cloth or wearing light clothes. This strengthens the whole body, because all the cells absorb the powers gratefully. These powers are also soothing for the eyes as well as serving to calm and strengthen the nerves.

*Cleansing the body should
also take place from within*

A cure with freshly squeezed elderberry juice purifies the whole organism. Drink two liqueur glasses a day.

Tea made of white deadnettle is very strengthening.

The white deadnettle can also be prepared with alcohol. It brings about inner strengthening and increased vitality. Pluck the dead nettle in the morning and then put it immediately into alcohol. You can use a normal glass jar for this purpose. Approximately four days before the full moon, put the jar on a windowsill at night, and during the day place it in a cool room, covered. The combination of alcohol and dead nettle blossoms attracts the moon particles, which are particularly heavily charged with energy during the nights before the full moon. After four days strain and drink daily 1-2 teaspoons. This strengthens and vitalizes the body. This extract can also be used for rubbing the body, especially the abdomen. The moon particles penetrate the abdominal organs and not only strengthen the entire abdomen, but also affect the ovaries, stimulating a strong and healthy ovum formation.

The red deadnettle is blood-building. It should be dried and used for tea.

Advice for scrofula and psoriasis

When suffering from scrofula, gather fern and lay it in the open air for several nights before the full moon. Then cut it into small pieces and prepare a bath with it twice a week.

If the feet tend to perspire, put fresh fern in your shoes, or put the feet on a bag filled with fern at night.

If you suffer from psoriasis, proceed as follows:

Put fresh leaves of the stinging nettle into alcohol, as described above. After 4-5 days, filter out the leaves, and rub the alcoholic substance into the scalp in the evening. The tender vessels of the scalp have a vibrational effect on the whole body. If the psoriasis has not improved after some time, you can rub the whole body with the substance. Thin it down a bit more beforehand. Remember that, at first, the Spirit treats only a part of the body and not the whole body right away. He knows the causes and from where they can be treated. People want to tackle the whole problem immediately. The Spirit builds up slowly and intensifies the treatment, as it is good for the soul and body.

In very mild cases of psoriasis, the same effect can be achieved by rinsing the head with freshly prepared tea of the stinging nettle. Rinse the head several times. You can also rub the entire body with the tea. During this treatment do not use chemical products to cleanse your body, but use curd soap. Do not use setting lotions, gels, sprays and the like, either. Instead of stinging nettle tea, you can use extract of pure chamomile.

Ulcers, wounds and burns

Brewer's yeast contributes to the healing of internal and external ulcers. You can take it internally or apply it to the wound, which you should protect with a piece of nettle cloth.

Wounds and external ulcers can be healed by ointment made of calendula. Cover the wound or ulcer thickly with ointment and protect it with a linen cloth.

For abscesses or external ulcers, a "drawing" ointment is helpful. Take coltsfoot, tormentil and plantain. Dry, pulverize, and mix them with vaseline. This ointment, made fresh frequently, can work wonders.

In case of burns, preferably put thick cream on the burnt skin. If this is not at hand, use rich milk or pure sunflower oil. Rub it carefully into the damaged skin until the pain recedes. Dab the wound, then apply approximately one millimeter of calendula ointment. If not available, vaseline can also be used.

PART 4

The Various Fragrances and Their Effects

Fragrances are also contained in the eternally divine ether, the life force and healing power. However, in this revelation of spiritual healing methods, I want to touch on the world of sensations of the fragrances only briefly:

The fragrance of sandalwood calms down the mind and makes one sensitive.

The fragrance of rosewood increases vitality and contributes to the formation of gastric juices.

Lavender activates the brain cells and vitalizes the whole organism.

The fragrance of myrrh helps a person to go into his inner being, thus contributing to internalization.

The fragrance of incense awakens the spiritual powers in a person. Incense also gives life force to the surroundings. Those invisible beings that do not set value on awakening the inner powers within them, turn away from the fragrance of incense.

The fragrance of columbine root strengthens the heart as well as the blood circulation. The smell of the root of stinging nettle strengthens the lungs.

The fragrance of the roots of elecampane, also called elfdock, and of wormwood calms down the gastric nerves.

The fragrances of the roots of violets and oxlip or key flower have a wholesome effect on the solar plexus.

The fragrances of peppermint root and sage root send healing forces to the liver and gall bladder.

The fragrance of marshmallow root activates the spleen.

The fragrances of elecampane and pimpernel activate the functions of the glands.

The fragrances of the root of silver-mantle and lady's-mantle send upbuilding and healing powers to the hormones.

The smell of the roots of broom and lesser centaury has a beneficial effect on the organs of women and men in the lower abdomen.

The fragrance of the root of small flowered willow herb strengthens the prostate gland. The fragrance of lily roots stimulates the whole organism.

All these fragrances should, however, be breathed in not too intensely, and not too often, only briefly in the morning and perhaps in the evening. It should be an agreeable and light fragrance.

Therefore, put the roots either into a little bowl with some water and put it on a fireplace or put the healing roots on a plate warmer.

The roots should neither be boiled nor singed, just warmed up slightly, until they release their fragrances.

Proceed in the same way as briefly mentioned above with myrrh and incense. Always take only a small quantity of them. Too much can have a negative effect.

PART 5

The Significance of Colors and Sounds and Their Effects on the Soul and the Person

Colors are energies. They can contribute to the success of a project as well as speeding up healing processes.

Colors influence a person's disposition. The energies flowing from colors can bring about a higher vitality, but can also cause depression.

Every nuance of color, whatever hue it may be, affects the soul and also the physical body.

The colors, forms and fragrances with which a person surrounds himself express his way of thinking and acting, his character. They are the mirror image of his soul.

Just as a person feels and thinks, he becomes.

A person with a good character and positive traits will wear light colors, especially if he walks the path to God. The person who is walking the path of the evolution of his consciousness refuses every gloomy color because his developing gift of high sensitivity tells him that dark colors do not balance and stimulate him, but rather depress him.

Disharmonious and dark colors have a low rate of vibration. These frequencies elicit physical discomfort and also change a person's looks. Nondescript colors like gray and black elicit neither joy nor comfort in a person.

A person's magnetic field is also influenced by colors.

The shade of color to which a person tends dominates his aspirations and thoughts.

Bright, that is, balanced and harmonious colors contribute to a positive stimulation and thus, to the healing of illnesses.

The laws of God express themselves in colors and forms. The majority of people know little about the great lawful correlations based on colors and shapes.

Hospital rooms, for instance, are unadorned, painted in colors that do not vitalize and are often simply gray and drab. The low vibration of these colors takes the last strength from some patients as well as the courage they still have to affirm their recovery and becoming healthy. On the other hand, bright, light colors and a pleasant environment give the patient rest, peace, help, and even have a healing effect.

Everything is based on vibration. Thus, every human being is dependent on his own rate of vibration as well as that of his surroundings. Therefore, every person should place great value on orderly conditions and a harmonious home. According to the law of the Lord, every human being should have pleasant surroundings and an appropriate home. This does not mean that he should revel in luxury. He should furnish his home in a way that brings him rest and peace. It should be a home full of warmth and harmony, where he can recover from the exertions of the day.

It behooves people in the affluent countries to provide their poorer fellowmen with a decent life and an adequate home. The law of "Pray and Work" applies to every citizen of the Earth, also for the people in the underdeveloped countries. If people in the overly rich countries would follow the commandments of unity and love for one's neighbor, there would also be work, bread and pleasant housing in the underdeveloped countries – though not in luxury, but comfortable moderateness. The law of the Lord says: The one helps carry the burden of the other. Therefore, people who have not had spiritual schoolings should be helped, that is, they should be given the possibility to work. Trade with other countries is also a part of this.

If humankind had actualized the divine laws, the press of souls toward incarnation would not be so great now, because they would have already reached their goal in a previous life. Consequently, there would be no overpopulation, because developed souls would turn to the divine goal and not be inclined to return to matter. The one who has not developed on this side of life in the sense of the Spirit and does not recognize the meaning and purpose of his life on Earth will aimlessly waste the days God has given him on Earth, disoriented and without self-control. The soul of a person who does not make use of the days in the sense of the Spirit and does not purify and cleanse himself in the Earth's school will not find a hold in God, its Father, once it is disincarnate, but will go again into a further incarnation. The population explosion is the result of the unenlightened state of former generations. The souls of many unknowing ancestors are again in an earthly garment and, just as in previous lives, they waste their precious time on Earth – a time that should be one of dawning awareness. The alternation of birth and death will continue to take place until the soul recognizes itself, and the person and soul walk the path to the higher self.

Therefore, O human being, make use of the time on Earth by recognizing your goal in life, the Spirit of God in you. Strive untiringly to ennoble your senses, to raise your soul, so that you become the image of your Father.

The one who recognizes the meaning and purpose of his life of Earth will ennoble his five senses and become a virtuous, honest person who supports and helps his fellowman in all things.

If people had been enlightened about the spiritual laws and correlations and were thus knowing, if they would know about the power and might of thoughts, and also knew about the effect of colors on the soul and disposition of their fellowman, the domiciles, hospital rooms and clinics would be healing spaces, which, through appropriate shades of color and aromatic fragrances, would contribute to stimulating the soul and the whole organism. Light, harmonious colors that are coordinated, as well as fragrances of nature are bearers of life and healing forces.

The person chooses the colors and forms for his clothes and home environment according to his state of consciousness and character. A spiritually awakened person who likes order will coordinate the colors with each other. An orderly person can often be recognized by his dynamism. He prefers – depending on his spiritual state of development – the color red, but also brown, the color of the Earth. A person who likes order is constantly active, to smooth out everything, to put things in order, to adjust and provide for everything. The color red, the dynamic element, can primarily be the color that, in accordance with his character, he especially loves.

Nevertheless, every characteristic can tend to one-sidedness and become dangerous if the person does not constantly monitor himself and does not develop further good and divine characteristics. Thus, the dynamic color red can drive a one-sided person to passion, aggression, wrong decisions and impulsive acts.

If a sensitive person surrounds himself with a lot of red color, he can develop a nervous condition. Weak nerves influence the whole organism.

Brown, the color of the Earth, can have a calming effect, but shows a certain spiritual limitation. The color of Earth is the bearer of matter. A person who tends toward matter will prefer the darker shades of brown. However, brown can tone down red and, in this combination, even have a somewhat harmonizing effect.

A person who responds strongly to red should be cautious in his life. He is excessively ambitious in his life and tends to a pathological compulsion for order, and finally, to strokes. These symptoms can be overcome by self-discipline, but also by the soothing color of light green, combined with brown. The color blue also has a balancing and harmonizing effect.

Light green has a balancing effect on the solar plexus as well as the whole nervous system.

Especially the living and bright colors of nature influence a person's disposition and can stimulate and balance every organ. The green of nature is particularly effective, balancing, and harmonizing, if it is interwoven with the golden rays of the sun. In this combination, two degrees of vibration influence the person, the healing power of the sun in connection with the soothing and balancing color green.

I want to again mention here that all Being, including matter, is based on vibration, and every body, the human being, in particular, is surrounded by a dynamic, magnetic field.

The magnetic field of a very impulsive person attracts restless and disharmonious vibrations. Such a person is in much danger and tends toward wrong decisions and depression, but also toward aggression. If this magnetic charge is discharged, either through an accumulation of heat or an outburst of rage, mental or physical conditions can develop.

Nervous persons, perhaps with a nervous heart disease or illnesses caused by weak nerves should favor the colors green or light blue.

A pale blue has a calming and relaxing effect on a nervous person and a creative effect on a level-headed person, especially when a pale gold shade is included.

The color blue is balancing, but can also stimulate an apathetic person and build him up mentally as well as physically, harmonizing him and conveying a balancing stimulation to him.

Aggressive people who tend toward depression at the same time, and go from one extreme to the other should also surround themselves with pale blue.

The highly vibrating powers of the blue sky have an especially balancing and harmonizing effect. The spiritual powers come into action primarily when a person's disposition is calm.

During the transition from one season to another, the blue sky in the morning and evening, interwoven with golden shades, has an especially balancing and stimulating effect, awakening the powers of the soul.

When a continent turns to the sun in the morning, the gold and blue colors of the sky are especially active and have a very strong effect on the person who is still in a calm state, provided he links with these forces. The same holds true in the evening, when a continent slowly turns away from the sun. Here, too, the blue sky, interwoven with gold, has a soothing effect and strengthens the nerves.

These mild golden rays of the sun, which mix softly with the vibrations of the blue sky, also have an intense effect on an emotionally ill or fatalistic person.

The colors of a person's clothes and home also have an effect on a person's magnetic field.

The clothes illustrate the character of the person. Not only is the favored color a reflection of the soul, but also the color combination and style of the clothes.

A person who prefers red up to dark red is not yet balanced. He is dynamic and very orderly, but also unpredictable.

A pale red to old rose illustrates the ennoblement of the soul.

A person who prefers these shades of color in his home should use them together with a golden shade, which softens and brings sunshine into one's mood.

Dark red in connection with black is a sign of hardness and the ability to assert oneself, which is not based on a spiritual foundation.

On the other hand, pale red or green, pale blue, white, pale violet, or warm brown indicate spiritual awakening. The brighter and the more harmonious the colors are, the more balanced the person is. In saying this, I do not refer to the creations of your fashion designers who dictate the colors to modern humankind. I rather think of a person who strives for refinement and inwardness, and selects the colors of his clothing according to his own sensations.

A person's choice of clothes and their colors, or the shapes and shades of color in his home correspond to the aura of his soul. A spiritually wise person recognizes a person's spiritual consciousness, his modesty, humbleness and spiritual open-mindedness by the colors of his clothing and his home.

A person weak in willpower should mainly surround himself with the colors blue and light green. Pale red is also recommended.

In the home, blue can be coordinated with golden shades and white.

Golden shades gentle a person. They express the radiance of the sun. White is the power of the primordial light.

When the frequencies of blue, gold and white are harmoniously coordinated with one another, they contribute not only to the salvation of the soul, but also to convalescence.

I want to emphatically stress here that a person must strive to ennoble his five senses and to ask for the inner healing power, as well. Only then, can the effect of the colors and their nuances be perceived. Colors, forms and also fragrances and sounds unfold their harmonizing and healing effect only when a person strives to lead a life that is willed by God. When someone striving for harmony and seeking healing does not endeavor to promote the salvation of his soul and of his life force, the vibrations of the colors and forms can have very little effect. Nor will fragrances vivify him. As with all things, so is it with colors, sounds and fragrances: It depends on a positive inner attitude.

The color green in connection with white, gold or silver for your room has a harmonizing effect. But these colors can also have a depressing effect, especially on a melancholy person.

However, if the person goes to a lake region or the ocean, the color green can bring out decisiveness and vigor. The energetic powers of the ocean or of the lakes have a stimulating effect in the morning as well as in the evening sun. In the morning they activate; in the evening they are calming.

Emerald green is the symbol of willpower. It conveys balanced decisiveness, because it is a spiritual elemental force. It is the power of the driving element and contains predominantly spiritual carrier atoms, which are also called spiritual stabilization atoms.

In the Spirit, bright blue is the bearer of Wisdom. This is likewise an elemental power, which consists mainly of spiritual atoms of creation, also called design and formation atoms. Therefore, blue is the color of artists and designers, insofar as they sense the inner breath of the eternal Spirit and walk on the divine path more than on the ways of this world.

Pale violet with a little bit of white, in connection with a balanced and light golden shade, brings out decisiveness and courage. This pale violet color is the expression of the divine consciousness in the nature of Earnestness.

Silver, bright shining white, and white-gold are, in turn, high divine powers that lend expression to the divine life.

These seven basic colors are very closely interwoven in the Spirit. All these colors of the divine natures and attributes are interwoven with each other and bathed in bright white, silver and white-gold, in the radiance that, in turn, expresses strength and constancy in its frequency.

I want to expressly point out that my revelations refer exclusively to colors and not to metal and the jewelry made of it in this world.

Once again, may it be indicated: If the colors in sickrooms were to be coordinated with those seeking recovery, much could be contributed to their convalescence simply by stimulating their disposition and calming their nerves. Colors, forms, sounds and, of course, fragrances, contribute to a balanced and harmonious life in a human being.

Your inner state shapes your external appearance. Your spiritual maturity is shown in colors and forms. The more ennobled a person's soul is, the brighter his clothes are and the simpler his behavior and his nature.

Your appearance is a reflection of your soul. A person who is spiritually wise and truly enlightened recognizes the character of a human being by his appearance, his behavior, his gestures, his manner of talking and, not least, by the colors of his clothing.

Many people think they can disguise themselves by pretending to be pious and balanced. The truly wise one cannot be deceived. He knows the characteristics of his fellow brothers and sisters and can classify them immediately, even when they behave and dress differently. The vibrations that a person emanates can be sensed and determined by anyone who rests in God. Without saying a word, he knows what kind of person he is dealing with.

The truly wise person is silent. The person who has only worldly knowledge thinks he must show off. He judges from the viewpoint of his own limited intellect.

The truly enlightened one will discern, but not speak about his perception, and then adjust to his neighbor's rate of vibration.

The eternal Spirit consists of an eternal energy field that permeates all life forms. The eternal Being, the expression of the Absolute, is a radiating white, a white-gold, eternal radiance. All forms of Being draw from its power.

Seven basic rays go out of this eternal field of energy and power. They bear all other colors in themselves. These seven bundles of rays are refracted by the prism suns.

Therefore, the divine rays of the law consist of seven times seven powers.

These seven times seven rays of the eternal Spirit are the inherent laws that brought forth all Being; they permeate, and maintain it.

Every divine ray has its particular shade of color and contributes to the harmonization of the whole.

According to this flowing and rhythmic law of seven times seven cosmic rays, the primordially eternal power is active in all ethereal forms, in the pure spirit beings and human beings, as well.

The spiritual suns of the eternal Being, with their fine-material planets and worlds, which consist of pure, yet compressed, ether, are the absolute expression of these seven times seven powers.

The ethereal forms of the pure spirit beings were also created by the eternal Spirit according to the immutable law of the seven times seven radiating powers.

The entirety of infinity rests on a spiritual atomic foundation, which is based on the seven times seven rays.

The eternal energy field of the Spirit is likewise in every soul. This incorruptible eternal power is called the divine spark or the core of being of the soul.

Once the soul has again regained its purity and become the image of God, it becomes an eternal ether body once again, which is one with the rhythm of the holy, eternally flowing law of God.

Seven prism suns are active in infinity. They refract the seven basic rays of the Spirit.

These prism powers are also active in every human being as consciousness centers. These spiritual-energetic prism bases are the spiritual organs of the soul, or – once the soul has gained absolute purity – of the ether body. The divine spark, the core of being, is the heart of the soul and of the ether body. The seven times seven rays, which flow from these seven prism powers, are the spiritual arteries of the eternal ether body, which also permeate its seven garments, the soul.

These seven times seven law powers, which consist of seven basic colors, also maintain the spiritual particle structure of the ether body, which lends the latter a spiritual form. The structure of the ether body is formed by the spiritual particles, which were created by the primordial Spirit from atoms of light ether. Within these spiritual vessels, the particles, further spiritual types of atoms are active. They absorb the light, the shades of color, of the seven times seven powers and reflect them.

The spiritual-divine circulation of the ether body is connected – by way of the core of being – to the great universal circulation and is fed from the energetic basis, the Primordial Central Sun. As long as the microcosm, the spiritual ether body, is in absolute harmony with the spiritual macrocosm, it is the law itself, since all pure Being is the spiritual-divine law.

The one who violates even one of these seven times seven lawful rays changes in himself the rate of vibration of the holy law, which is based on the seven times seven powers and which consists of the seven basic nuances of color.

Since one of the spirit beings wanted to be like God, the Fall began, which initiated the Fall of the angels. In the ether bodies of all those spirit beings, which endorsed the rebellion of this one angel, the seven times seven cosmic powers changed. The result was that the spirit beings could no longer be the image of God, since they no longer lived and acted according to the law of the seven times seven powers, but strove toward unlawfulness, namely, to be like God. Through this unlawful act, they changed their ether structure more and more. With their thoughts, which entailed their self-will and their arbitrary actions, they created their own criteria and devised privileges, which became their characteristics.

It is the law: The one who violates the law of the Lord, the seven times seven rays or powers, surrounds himself with his own aura. In its broadest sense, the result was that the core of being, the divine spark, drew these seven times seven law powers closer to itself, since the spirits of the opposition no longer asked for them.

The same immutable law is also valid for human beings: If a person does not live according to the holy powers of the law, these can become effective in the person, in his cells, glands, organs and hormones only to a diminished extent. In the same measure as the core of being withdraws its pure cosmic powers, souls and human beings envelop themselves with their own aura, with their self-taught characteristics, which shape their character.

With their ever stronger disregard of the law, the seven reversely polarized characteristics of the Fall-beings formed seven garments around the pure ether body, and over the course of time, the strongest crystallization, the human being. These seven garments of the ether body, called the soul, produce in the person the seven consciousness centers with their different shades of color.

The one who does not live according to the laws of God disturbs the interaction of the seven times seven energetic powers that are expressed with colors. Whatever is not identical to the eternally harmonious divine law disturbs itself and its environment, as well.

The more a person changes these seven times seven powers – which want to flow as lawful principles in his body and influence every cell of his body – with a wrong way of thinking, speaking and acting, thus causing disharmony, the more intensely he builds on the structure of his fate. If these seven times seven colors are no longer in harmony with the Infinite, that is, if the shades of color of one of the seven consciousness centers deviate greatly from the corresponding cosmic law-color, the forces coming from a wrong, human way of thinking and acting have a negative effect on the entire organism.

The seven consciousness centers are the mirror image of the soul as well as of the body. Their radiation forms the aura of the human being. Every vibration has a certain frequency and color, which are reflected in the particle-structure of your spirit body and in your soul, as well as in your physical body.

The human being is the reflection of his way of thinking and acting. Every illness is the effect of a cause, which changed the seven times seven law-rays in the person. Your troubles, blows of fate and sorrows, too, are evoked solely by your world of thoughts, since every thought is a force that returns to you. If your thoughts are disharmonious, even evil, you change the shades of color of your seven consciousness centers according to your way of thinking and acting.

Every color of the Spirit is based on spiritual atoms, which change through negative thoughts and actions, resulting in a confused radiation, which influences your soul and the organism as well. The darker, less harmonious and more confused these seven times seven powers of the consciousness centers are, the more dangerous it is for the human being. Sooner or later, these disharmonious powers will have an effect in your body.

An inner tension, often caused by the friction of disharmonious frequencies, always sets off a blow of fate. The state of your consciousness centers is the result of the forces generated by your thoughts. If the colors of the consciousness centers are bright and in harmony with the colors of the divine law, then person and soul are also balanced and healthy.

Every person should therefore memorize the following basic principles, and repeat them again and again:

Your sensations, your thoughts, words, and deeds shape your personality.

All impure, unlawful sensations and patterns of thinking, speaking and acting are building blocks on the structure of your fate. You, bring into harmony the seven times seven powers in you. May your feelings and your patterns of thinking and acting become pure and in accordance with the seven times seven law powers. Then, you will become healthy and live in harmony and peace.

Recognize that harmonious, bright colors, beautiful and well-balanced forms, light, natural fragrances and harmonious sounds contribute to the combination of harmonious colors in your inner being, in soul and body.

As long as the human being lets himself drift in the ocean of this world, without steering toward the rescuing shore, the law of God, he will be or become a person adrift.

With the disharmonious workings of his inner forces, a person will suffer terribly in this life or in one of the next ones. Everything that the human being does not recognize and repent of, the soul takes with it to one of the worlds of the beyond, which corresponds to the degree of vibration of its acquired characteristics.

The shades of color of the seven power centers of the soul indicate the state of your consciousness. These seven consciousness powers form the seven garments of your shadowed ether body, your soul.

What a person does not clear up in this life will come back to him, either in one of his next incarnations or in the soul realms. The structure of your fate will collapse and fall in over you if you do not recognize it in time. This means, if you do not recognize yourself and, through a pure, lawful life, carry away one stone of fate after the other. This is accomplished by the person purifying himself with a corresponding life, harmonizing the seven powers, and adjusting them to God's consciousness, the eternal, incorruptible and lawful energy field of the Spirit.

Recognize that all instructions given in this book can contribute to the purification of your soul and the harmonization of your body.

Only through a harmoniously stimulating balance of colors of your consciousness, will you come into higher vibration and into the evolution of your consciousness, which will give you health, happiness and joy in life.

Bright, harmonious powers are the powers of God. Therefore, O human being, act according to the law of the Lord. Ennoble your thinking and acting and surround yourself with bright, harmonious colors, forms, and sounds, then your soul and body will become light-filled. When the eye is bright, your body will also be filled with light.

Now, I will give a brief revelation about the effects of sound on soul and body.

If the sounding board of a person, the soul, has been schooled by the eternal Spirit, that is, if it has attained a high degree of purification, the person becomes tranquil and turned within.

All disharmonious sounds are painful and burdensome for the sounding board, the soul. This can already be recognized by a person's manner of speaking. Hasty and uncontrolled talking points to a restless, burdened, and tense soul. Restlessness, no matter what kind, is not divine, and interrupts the holy stream, the law of the Lord.

In a spiritually developed person, the harmony of his mature and developed soul is expressed in all things. His flow of speech is calm, his manner of speaking, harmonious and purposeful. He is likable and speaks only very little. However, when he talks, it is with purposeful words that express only the essential. A person of the Spirit knows about the fundamental things of life. He knows that every disharmonious and too-loud word damages the sounding board, the soul. Every disharmonious gesture is, in turn, the expression of a still tense soul that is oriented to without.

Loud and shrill sounds hinder the soul from perceiving the Spirit, which is prepared at every moment to give His child the necessary, lawful instructions.

The one who surrounds himself with disharmonious sounds can no longer perceive the harmonious, soft voice of God and its guidance, because soul and person are not attuned and tend to reject the quiet powers of the Spirit rather than encourage them.

The human being is, at the same time, transmitter and receiver. If he does not orient his antenna to the harmonious melodies of the divine and does not switch his thoughts and actions over to the divine, he will not perceive this soft, divine voice. His antenna, as well as his receiver are oriented to the world, causing him to receive more and more dissonances and negativity and, in turn, to emit them.

Sounds of whistles and shrill, screeching loud music are unimaginably disruptive elements for the soul as well as for the physical body.

If a person wants to obtain inner calm and harmony, it is essential that he strive to bring the shell of his soul, his physical body, into harmony. This harmony, which is acquired little by little, then has an effect on the motor, the soul, which slowly aligns with the rhythmically flowing power-stream of the Spirit of God in the core of being or divine spark.

I repeat: Every disharmonious sound has a disruptive effect on the soul as well as on the physical body.

A person who continuously lives in a field of disharmonious sounds cannot spiritually grow and become healthy. In the disharmonious field of this world, he will become a sick, haggard little plant that is stricken by all manner of illnesses. Such a little plant, which can find only scanty food in the poor field, will infect many unknowing people turned to without, and with them, spread further unrest.

Disharmoniously loud, fiery and rhythmic sounds are considerable pathogens. It is not seldom that they contribute to the encouragement of the most terrible disease, cancer.

Just as negative thoughts, words and disharmonious colors, disharmonious sounds and tones likewise disturb the magnetic field of your soul and build onto the structure of your fate.

The seven times seven holy rays are the symphonies of the Spirit. These holy powers permeate the seven times seven heavenly spheres and fashion the music of the heavenly spheres.*

I repeat, so that humankind may memorize it well:
Loud, shrill sounds and fiery music disturb the delicate vibrations of the ether body, just as unlawful sensations, thoughts and actions. This causes the soul to become restless and tense, and soul and person fall ill.

---

* Note: The music of the heavenly spheres is the eternally radiating primordial sensation of the All-Spirit. It is harmony, spiritually manifest: the stillness.

People's blows of fate and suffering are the effect of causes that are based on a wrong way of thinking, speaking and acting, but also on disharmonious colors, forms, fragrances and sounds.

The Lord of eternal life sent into this world gifted beings, who, in the earthly garment, conveyed harmonious sounds to His people. Many of these melodies and tunes are reminiscent of the heavenly sounds of the law, of the divine music of the spheres.

Soft, mellifluous and harmonious melodies, especially those brought out by mandolins, flutes, violins and above all, harps, are almost like the heavenly music of the spheres. These melodies can contribute significantly to harmonizing a person and his soul.

Sounds also trigger vibrations that affect one or the other of the seven consciousness centers, depending on their frequency.

In your innermost being, in the seven consciousness centers, and also in your body, every unlawful sound produces dissonances, which disturb the function of the cells, organs, glands, hormones and also your nervous system. The whole organism is impaired in its function by these unlawful sounds. The result of these causes can be illness.

Recognize, O human being: mellifluous and harmonious melodies promote your health and can contribute to a speedier recovery. Therefore, know that whatsoever you surround yourself with, you are, or you will become.

PART 6

To Attain Spiritual Evolution, a Life According to the Laws of the Lord Is Necessary –

Summary of the most important laws of God revealed in this book

The one who unfolds the holy ether powers, the Spirit, by leading a lawful life will attain health, inner joy, happiness and harmony according to the will of the Lord.

The commandment of all commandments, which carries the entire divine law, is love. Therefore, it is written: "Love God, your Lord and Father, with all your heart, with all your strength, and your neighbor as yourself."

However, you can love God, our Lord, with all your heart and with all your strength only if you can love your fellowman.

The Spirit of God is in all Being and especially in His perfect child. Therefore, you should recognize, accept and love your neighbor as the image of God.

Even though a person may not be faultless in his manner of thinking and acting, no one has the right to judge him, by thinking and talking about him, denying all the good aspects that his neighbor also has. Such impure conduct burdens the person; for it does not contribute to unity and thus, not to the fulfillment of the divine law, either. To fulfill the law, one has to recognize that each person must answer only to God, our Lord in Christ, for his way of thinking and acting.

What does a person gain by saying negative things about his brother or even doing them to him? The one who judges will be judged, and his brother gets no help from this.

If you really want to help and support your neighbor, actualize the words of the Lord: "See first the beam in your own eye and remove it." Only then, once you have removed it, can you lawfully help to remove the splinter from the eye of your brother.

The same is true if you want to lead a healthy, happy and peaceful life, joyful in God, which safeguards you from illness, sorrow, need and blows of fate. First of all, see the beam in your own eye. This means that as long as you do not constantly monitor yourself, in order to thereby gradually fulfill and keep the laws of the Lord, you will be below the almighty divine law. Only when you yourself have become the law, a pure child of the heavens, will you feel, think, speak and act out of the purest love for God and for your neighbor. Without fulfillment of the holy laws of God, there is no freedom from illness, need, tribulation and worry. It is solely the fulfillment of the laws of the Lord that will make a person free. If the human being is still below the law, that is, if he does not yet think and act according to the laws of God, he will create causes again and again, which, in turn, will bring about their effects.

To escape the wheel of cause and effect, it is necessary to know and fulfill the seven basic levels of the divine law. This begins with the level of Order and ends on the level of the divine Mercy.

*Every soul must complete
the seven basic levels of the Spirit*

The basic levels of the Spirit, the law of the Lord, which every soul has to go through, are, individually: ORDER, WILL, WISDOM, EARNESTNESS, PATIENCE, LOVE and MERCY.

All these divine basic levels also have their sub-levels. This means that every basic level is contained, in turn, in the other basic levels as a sub-level. All seven basic levels have their particular, unchangeable rates of vibration and colors. Thus, there are seven times seven spheres of the law, also called basic heavens. Each of these seven basic heavens also vibrates in every other basic heaven as a sub-region. For instance, in the basic heaven of Love are also the levels of Order, Will, etc.

My endeavor is to reveal these seven basic heavens as a ladder of the law, so that the reader and the God-conscious person who walks the stepwise path to self-recognition can orient himself more easily. Provided a person wants to actualize the absolute love for God and divest himself of all human weaknesses and worries, may he heed the ladder of the law, the steps of the law.

If you want to walk the path to inner bliss and the solution to all your problems, start at the level of divine Order. Examine your thinking and acting and surrender your human habits to God, your Lord, so that He can lead and guide you, and you lose your human ego, little by little. Only once a person relinquishes his ego will he experience the divine power, the unlimited, eternally loving and helpful law of God. This inner power, the guide and healer of soul and person, gives itself to the child that is turned toward it, and causes its powers to flow throughout the soul as well as the person. Therefore, O human being, long for the fulfillment of the divine laws and strive continuously to fulfill the will of the Lord.

Order

Put your life in O r d e r : Examine and monitor your thoughts and words. Never talk negatively about your neighbor, but recognize that everything your neighbor says and does concerns only God and His child, and not you. Through negative thinking and acting, you only harm yourself, because a person will reap what he sows. For instance, if your neighbor's behavior irritates you, unlawful thoughts are already clinging to you. Examine yourself! Ask yourself whether you are always enjoyable for every person. Relate your sensations, thoughts and words that you pour over another to yourself! Ask yourself whether you are better!

When, through this constant self-analysis, you get to know yourself better, you will soon feel ashamed of yourself!

By practicing this self-analysis, you will condemn your neighbor in your thoughts, words and actions less and less, because you will become aware of the beam in your own eye. With this continuous monitoring of yourself, you will recognize very soon what a heavy beam is in your own eye.

Only good things should come from your heart and over your lips!

Once you have learned to curb yourself, you will also notice that any restlessness emanating from you causes disharmony, unhappiness, indisposition or illness in you. A way of thinking and acting that is not divine and lawful inevitably evokes manifold human trouble and suffering. These causalities, which the person initiates and which lead to inestimable effects, are not in the will of God. God, our Lord, allows the effects, so that via self-recognition, a person may attain the experience of God and strive for a lawful way of thinking and acting.

Therefore, O human being, ennoble your five senses on each of the seven basic levels, by recognizing your base inclinations and passions and curbing them. In this way, you will soon feel the divine powers that guide you and vivify your soul and your body, as well.

Recognize: Your soul is the motor of your body. Your body is the chassis. The fuel is the eternal Spirit, the core of being of your soul.

If a person does not orient himself to the eternally, harmoniously flowing Spirit, the all-permeating divine ether, by leading a God-filled, lawful life, he causes contrary vibrations between spirit, soul and body.

If someone violates the divine laws, by feeling, thinking and acting unlawfully, the motor and the chassis, that is, the soul and person, become disharmonious. Every hate-filled thought or every malicious word, even every disharmonious gesture, brings the soul as well as the body into upheaval. These violations of the law cause unlawful forces to come up in a person, which debilitate his soul and physical body. Restlessness, haste, all forms of indisposition and illness mentioned above develop, because with base inclinations and compulsions, the person poisons soul and body, the motor and the chassis, with the fuel of base thoughts, words and deeds, that is, with unlawful forces.

Self-serving, egotistic, impure thoughts and actions cause the Spirit of God, the divine fuel of your soul, to withdraw more and more, in order to leave free will to His child.

Will

Recognize that the divine W i l l makes a person free.

Once the person has learned to get his feelings, thoughts, words and actions under control, he should also consider his will. Practice recognizing the divine Will. Strive to ask for God's guidance every morning and place your will under the Will of your heavenly

Father. Check your manner of speaking; it should be harmonious and balanced. Separate non-essential from essential. Watch yourself: Do your sentences still sound like the following: "I want this or that" or "This or that should be guided or steered in a different way"? This argumentation of your egotistic human ego impels your motor, the soul, and also your chassis, to unlawful activity and accomplishment.

Recognize that the Spirit of God does not support your self-will. Your constant tendency to act according to your self-will continously saps your mental and physical powers!

A person does not immediately perceive the negativity building up in his body. The result of human striving for wanting to be and to have are spiritual and physical tensions that lead to depression, which burdens your nerves and weakens your organs. Every unlawful way of feeling and acting results in disharmony. The low rate of vibration of your soul and body resulting from this creates causes that are followed by their effects.

Therefore, O human being, feel, think and speak in a divine way! Strive to fulfill the Will of God and ask every day anew that He, the Lord, guide you, His child.

Work in full harmony, even when your colleagues pressure you and want to transmit their hectic manner to you.

Try to be above the worldly things that bring out haste, hardship and misery.

Do not carry out your daily duties in restlessness and haste. Be *above* these things and then they will serve you.

Don't push to get this and that done today no matter what. Work calmly but with purpose, in order to do justice to all people and tasks in accordance with the Will of God.

If your brother is angry because you could not complete a seemingly important task today, do not be upset with him. If you have fulfilled your daily tasks conscientiously, you can rest assured that God's omnipotence and love can also bring out understanding in your angry fellowman and calm him down, so that he may become understanding. He will then be content to wait until tomorrow when his desires will certainly be fulfilled. God, your Lord, is almighty. Trust in Him, and you will truly become a spiritually wise person.

Wisdom

The W i s d o m of God is the deed, the shaping element.

Ask daily for wisdom, as well. When you know that all your feelings, thoughts, words, actions, and your self-will is under God's care, His Wisdom will lend you wings. You will work more quickly because you are calm and turned within. You have learned to let yourself be guided by the inner fuel, the core of being of your soul. The fuel in you, the divine power, will increase and you will become the glove on God's hand.

He, the Lord, the true, omniscient energy of your soul and of your physical body will know how to guide you in such a way that you can achieve more each day in total harmony and calmness than your colleagues can ever do working in their stress and in a hectic manner. The work you have accomplished will be good and worthy of praise. Through your nearness to God, you will become a calm and radiating pole for your colleagues and, thanks to your inner guidance, be able to support them with advice and help.

By constantly monitoring and examining yourself, you have learned to be above the things of this world. However, you should always be friendly toward your fellowman and ready to help him. Never put yourself above your neighbor. A truly spiritually wise person will not do this, since he knows of his own struggles with himself. The inner strength, the power of infinity, which guides you and gives you everything that can be of benefit to you, will again and again let you feel and recognize that a truly spiritually wise person serves his neighbor to the extent that his neighbor's consciousness has developed.

Earnestness

The divine E a r n e s t n e s s lets you recognize your impure habits. The inner stillness, which you achieved by leading a life of devotion, enables your soul and your physical body to experience the earnestness of life. By virtue of this constant guidance by the inner Spirit, you will become a good observer of your surroundings.

The divine Earnestness, which streams from the fourth basic level of your consciousness, brings your own faults and weaknesses before you again and again. Since you have achieved spiritual maturity, you will also recognize the faults and weaknesses of your fellowman in a lawful way. Especially by way of this basic level of Earnestness, you may experience and perceive the needs, weaknesses and also struggles of your fellowman.

Through this constant schooling by the Spirit, you will become a merciful person, who can support all people according to their spiritual recognitions. You, as an upwardly striving spiritual person, will feel health in yourself and a growing spiritual joy in life. Your small human ego, which wants to drag you down again and again, diminishes more and more.

Selflessness, understanding and the willingness and courage to make sacrifices replace your egocentric way of thinking and striving. In this way, your soul as well as your physical body receive increased divine powers. You will learn, little by little, to guide these gifts of salvation according to the law. Through extensive recognitions, which are based on the absolute divine law, you will attain the power of self-healing in the name of the Inner Physician and Healer.

Patience

Equipped with these selfless gifts of the Spirit, you enter the fifth level: P a t i e n c e.

A person who is climbing the spiritual ladder has learned to practice patience with himself. This patience and tranquility will irradiate from him and he will know how to convey it to his neighbor.

Through the increased divine gifts of Wisdom, the upward striving person has learned to be above worldly habits. His body obeys him for the most part.

In this way, the person striving for God will become a sensitive person who grasps a situation immediately. This enables him to help his fellowman to bear his troubles and sorrows more easily.

On the steps of recognition leading to the higher self, the willing pupil has practiced supporting his neighbor and giving advice, if it is asked for.

A spiritually persevering and knowing person who is intent on fulfilling the laws of God will not, however, force his spiritual and worldly knowledge on his neighbor. He will talk to him and discuss his neighbor's concerns according to the consciousness level of the latter. He will cautiously bring to his unknowing fellowman an understanding of where the causes for his troubles and illnesses could lie and how he can treat or eliminate them.

The spiritual pupil has experienced on himself all the conditions of his fellowmen. He knows how difficult and lengthy it can often be until a person comprehends how the omnipotence and love of God can work.

Love

On the sixth level, the person then awakens to selfless, divine L o v e , which wants to sacrifice itself for its fellowman.

The assiduous and divinely wise one experiences to a greater measure the outpouring of divine Love, which lets him become the bearer of all that is good.

The ever-flowing Love of God will give itself abundantly to the devoted child. In this way, the spiritually wise person will draw nearer and nearer to the eternal almighty One. He, the Lord of all life, the Spirit of God, can also help His upward striving child to worldly advancement and success and place His child in a high worldly position so that it can set a radiant example for many subordinates.

Recognize this, O human being, and take care not to fall back by becoming egotistical and selfish because of your high position. Strive to serve your fellowman at all times.

If God, the Lord, has put you in a high position in this world, because you have attained a spiritually high degree of consciousness, then know that you should be the least among those close to you and also among your subordinates. Respect and esteem your neighbor, whatever work he might be doing. Continue to practice neighborly love and know that God wants to work on your neighbor, His child, through you.

Mercy

The eternally glorious Spirit then leads you to the seventh level, M e r c y .

Be a Samaritan! A true, divinely wise person strives to walk untiringly at God's hand, and to never move away from the radiating light of His glory. In this way, he can never be led astray.

A person who has consciously turned toward the divine, who has become the glove on God's hand, recognizes and grasps much more quickly than a worldly individual what lies ahead. A divinely wise, enlightened person sees through his subordinates, and will know how to guide them with a righteous and just hand. He has, himself, experienced the Spirit's guidance on every level of the law. Through the divine power effective in him, he will know how to guide his subordinates. Such a person will act wisely and guide his fellowmen in a way that is good and lawful.

By virtue of the degree of maturity that the enlightened person has attained by way of the divine help – because he has untiringly subjected himself to self-monitoring and still does – he knows to what level of consciousness he has to adapt in order to clarify things for his neighbor and instruct him.

Just as God, the Lord, guided him, he is also called upon to instruct and guide his subordinates regarding the seven basic levels of life. Since the Spirit of God is very close to him, he will be given the strength to act appropriately. He will know how to guide his neighbor wisely without hurting him, so that he may become a productive person and co-worker.

Recognize, O human being: the seven basic levels are the path of the dawning consciousness of your soul and your human being.

If you walk this path step by step, you will attain health, inner joy, peace, harmony and selflessness.

Everything that you are not successful in today, you will master later, in accordance with God's will and counsel. Once the Spirit of God has become your vivifying life, He will give you all that you need, not only spiritually, but also physically. The power of the Holy Spirit can place you in the blessed position, in which you can attain all the material things of this world. Beware, however, that you do not consider this as your property. Of everything that you receive, give a part to your neighbor and continue to set an example for those around you so that they can learn from you. God, the Lord, has put you in this position so that you may be a radiant light in the darkness.

The Spirit of God knows only health and spiritual joy in life. On the ladder to recognition, practice love for God and neighbor. Then the Spirit of God will give you all you need for your further spiritual and worldly progress.

Spirit-teacher Brother Emanuel, the Cherub of divine Wisdom, wishes all his brothers and sisters in the earthly garment a blessed life and the fullness from the divine omnipotence.

Greetings in God!

Consciousness Centers

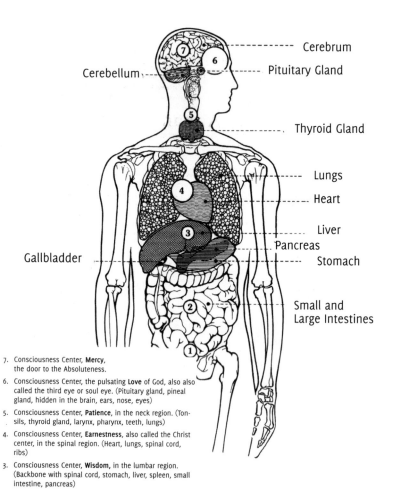

7. Consciousness Center, **Mercy**, the door to the Absoluteness.

6. Consciousness Center, the pulsating **Love** of God, also also called the third eye or soul eye. (Pituitary gland, pineal gland, hidden in the brain, ears, nose, eyes)

5. Consciousness Center, **Patience**, in the neck region. (Tonsils, thyroid gland, larynx, pharynx, teeth, lungs)

4. Consciousness Center, **Earnestness**, also called the Christ center, in the spinal region. (Heart, lungs, spinal cord, ribs)

3. Consciousness Center, **Wisdom**, in the lumbar region. (Backbone with spinal cord, stomach, liver, spleen, small intestine, pancreas)

2. Consciousness Center, **Will**, in the sacral region. (Kidneys with ureter, rectum, large intestine)

1. Consciousness Center, **Order**, in the coccyx region. (Iliac crest with hip joints, bladder, reproductive organs)

Consciousness Centers

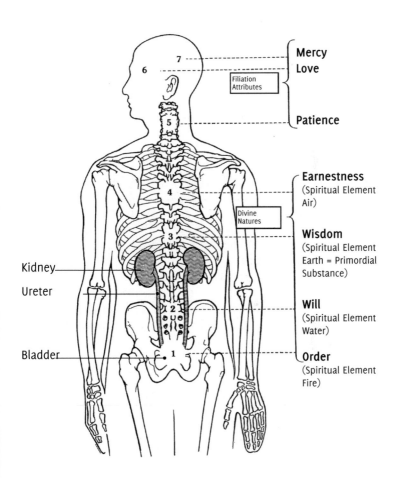

INDEX of HERBS and their LATIN NOMENCLATURE

alder buckhorn bark ...... Rhamnus frangula
balm mint ...... Melissa officinalis
barberry ...... Berberis vulgaris
bedstraw ...... Galium verum
broad-leaved or common plantain ...... Plantago major
broom roots ...... Genista pilosa
calendula ...... Calendula officinalis
celandine ...... Chelidonium majus
chamomile ...... Chamaemelum nobile
coltsfoot ...... Tussilágo fárfara
columbine ...... Aquilegia vulgaris
comfrey ...... Symphytum officinale
dandelion ...... Taraxacum officinale
dwarf mountain pine ...... Pinus mugo
early purple orchid ...... Orchis mascula
elecampane, also called elf dock ...... Inula helenium
five-leaf grass ...... Potentilla reptans
gentian ...... Gentiana lutea
hemp nettle ...... Galeopsis tetrahit
hops ...... Humulus lupulus
horsetail ...... Equisetum arvense
lady mantle ...... Alchemilla vulgaris
lavender ...... Lavandula Officinalis
lawn daisy ...... Béllis perénnis
lemon balm ...... Melissa officinalis
lesser centaury ...... Erythraea centaurium
lovage ...... Levisticum officinale
lungwort ...... Pulmonaria officinalis
marshmallow ...... Althaea officinalis
mistletoe ...... Viscum album

mistletoe	Viscum album
motherwort	Leonurus cardiaca
oat straw	Avena sativa
oxlip or key flower	Primula officinalis or Primula elatior
red deadnettle	Lamium purpurea
red pimpernel	Anagallis arvensis
ribwort, also called buckthorn, plantain	Plantago lanceolata
sage	Salvia
silver-mantle	Alchemilla alpina
silverweed, also called cinquefoil	Potentilla anserina
St. John's Wort	Hypericum perforatum
stinging nettle	Úrtica diócà
tormentil, also called erect cinquefoil	Potentilla erecta
vervain	Verbena officinalis
violets	Viola
white deadnettle	Lámium álbum
white hawthorn	Crataegus
wild chicory	Cichorium intybus
willow herb	Epilobium parviflorum
wormwood	Artemisia absinthium
yarrow	Aachilléa millefólium

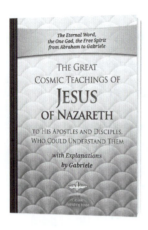

The Great Cosmic Teachings of JESUS of Nazareth
to His Apostles and Disciples, who could understand them
with Explanations by Gabriele

Through Gabriele, the great teaching prophetess and emissary of the Kingdom of God in our time, Christ himself reveals the law of a true life, which He taught more than 2000 years ago to the inner circle of His apostles and disciples. For the first time in the history of humankind, His great cosmic teachings are available to all people.

The great cosmic teachings help us understand the eternal divine laws and let us feel into the life that is deep in our soul, that is our homeland. In this way, we learn about who we truly are – cosmic beings, children of the unending love, and that we are on the way back to the eternal Kingdom of God, from where we once left.

The Great Cosmic Teachings of Jesus of Nazareth have been interpreted and explained by Gabriele. She shows us how we can apply them in our daily life, in the family, at work and in our free time.

The great cosmic teachings of Jesus of Nazareth have been compiled together with all the explanations by Gabriele in a large, nobly designed collective volume.

880 pp., HB, Order No. S 181en
ISBN 978-3-89201-951-0. $ 34.90
www.gabriele-publishing-house.com
Toll Free Order No.: 001-844-576-0937

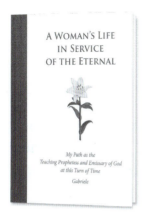

A Woman's Life in Service of the Eternal

My Path as the Teaching Prophetess and Emissary of God at this Turn of Time
Gabriele

For over 40 years, Gabriele serves God, the Eternal, as His teaching prophetess and emissary. In her autobiographical descriptions, she gives insight into her development as a human being and into her calling to become the prophetess of God, and what it means to bring His word, His love and wisdom to the Earth in our time.

From the desire to help and be a support to others with all that she has experienced and lived through, Gabriele allows the reader to take part in her life as a woman in service of the Eternal. Gabriele vividly describes the experiences in her life from early childhood on. She describes the beginnings of the prophetic word, the direct training she received from the Spirit of God and the build-up of the worldwide work of the Christ of God. She describes the deep joy of being one with God, our eternal Father, and likewise about the adversities and attacks, which she had to withstand, as a woman in service of the Eternal.

At the end of the autobiographical descriptions, contemporaries give a brief insight into the substantial creative power of Gabriele and the superhuman effort Gabriele made and still makes in her life for the Kingdom of God, for her fellowman, for all souls, indeed, for the entire creation of God.

204 pp., HB, Order No. S 551en,
ISBN 978-3-89201-814-8. $ 20.00

The Soul on Its Path to Perfection

The Christ of God reveals details about the development and structure of the eternal creation of the Being and about our soul through Gabriele, the prophetess and emissary of God in our time. Christ explains about the seven levels of consciousness of the soul and how they can be activated again – the task of every soul, whether on Earth or in the spheres of the beyond. Answers to many questions are given, for instance: What does the soul have to learn on each level? What about a soul that left its body at a young age? How does a soul live in the spheres of the beyond? And much more...

112 pp., Order No. S 209en, **$ 12.90, ISBN: 978-3-89201-952-7**

The Inner Physician and Healer

Become whole in soul and body, by the power of the Christ of God

The power of healing lies in tranquility

CD 1 & 2: The Inner Physician and Healer is the healing force in your soul • The Spirit of the Christ of God is effective in and through your breathing.   CD 1 & 2, 70 min., No. D 938en. **$ 15.00**

CD 3 & 4: The inner light radiates in and through your soul into your body • The eternal love, the sun of the primordial Being, gives and gives.   CD 3 & 4, 97 min., No. D 939en. **$ 15.00**

CD 5 & 6: Soul-searching and self-analysis guide us to ourselves • As we are the temple of God, God is the omnipresent eternal health in us.   CD 5 & 6, 97 min., No. D 940en. **$ 15.00**

This Is My Word
Alpha & Omega

The Gospel of Jesus
The Christ-Revelation which true Christians the world over have come to know

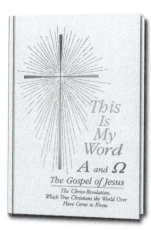

Who, truly, was Jesus of Nazareth? How can we know what He really taught? What were the facts about His life and teaching? This revelation of Christ goes beyond the contents of the Bible and gives answer to all the fundamental questions of our life today. And, it gives us a preview of the future and of the times to come in His Kingdom of Peace on the Earth.

Based on an apocryphal gospel called "The Gospel of Jesus," Christ himself gives previously unknown details about His incarnation in Jesus of Nazareth, conveyed by way of Gabriele, the prophetess and emissary of God for our time.

From the Contents: Infancy and youth of Jesus • The falsification of the teachings of Jesus over the past 2000 years • Meaning and purpose of our life on Earth • The law of Cause and Effect • Prerequisites for the healing of the body • The equality of men and women • God never punishes or condemns • The teaching of "eternal damnation" is a mockery of God • Jesus loved the animals and always supported them in their need • About death, reincarnation and life • The true meaning of the deed of redemption of Jesus, the Christ ... and much more.

1078 pp., SB, Order No. S 007en,
ISBN: 978-3-890841-38-6, $ 15.00
With a short autobiography of Gabriele

We will be glad to send you
our current catalog of our books,
CDs and DVDs, as well as free excerpts
of our books on many different topics.

Gabriele Publishing House – The Word
P.O. Box 2221 Deering, NH 03244, USA
Toll-Free Order No.: 001-844-576-0937
or:
Gabriele Publishing House – The Word
Max-Braun-Str. 02, 97828 Marktheidenfeld, Germany
Order No.: +49.9391-504-843
www.Gabriele-Publishing-House.com